Disclaimer

living or dead, or actual events is purely
coincidental.

ROYAL CREEK PUBLISHING HOUSE 2021

Chapter One

Osborne

Now

Michael Osborne exhaled.

The worst part about the waiting was the sweat. The world went on with life, unaware of what was about to come next, but Michael had to endure the profuse sweating. What he was doing could not be rushed in any way. So, he waited for the perfect opportunity.

The window through which he secretly sat looking, the lens on his sniper rifle providing a perfect, zoomed-in view of the crowd below, was on the fifth floor. Weston Hotel was the right kind of luxurious; not too opulent, neither too close to four-star. Michael had become quite accustomed to luxury ever since his investment firm, Osborne Investments, had kicked off the launch pad. He had had to deal with only a few months' worth of struggle. It had been pools of money for him after that.

Adjusting the lens, he took a look at the crowd once again—no sign of his target. There wouldn't be any until another thirty minutes, he figured. That was the deal with these people; they kept the public waiting longer than necessary. It was an inactive show of power, something they did to keep their egos fed and the people in line.

The cool of the rifle reminded him of perhaps some other life he had lived. It was foreign, the feeling. Or at least it felt foreign. Yet it had only been two years—two years ever since he had let his past self disappear in an unreachable abyss; two years since he had changed his identity and left his family and all of their sins.

And his sins.

He could not sit any longer waiting for the car to show up. He knew it would not be here in at least twenty minutes. He was damn sure. Getting up from his crouch, he quietly, invisible to the outside world, went outside the room he had been in. His suite was perfect. He had booked it under yet another name, wearing a third shade of hair and clothes no one would be able to recognize him in.

He entered his bedroom next, heading to the minibar. He sat, opened the door, and took his forever favorite: Vodka. Undoing the lid and downing the bottle's contents, he could not help but ruminate on the past.

Life as a Morano had been barbaric.

The Morano's were a formidable family. No other, not even the bloodthirsty Giovannis, sold on their territory. It all began when he got word of Tommy Giovanni, his arch-enemy, selling on Morano turf. What was more was that he had sold to only one kid in particular; a Patrick Monello. Michael's Patrick Monello.

Monello had been like a kid brother to Michael. They had met at the park when

Patrick was having trouble with some older bullying kids who would not let him have his turn on the seesaw. Michael had intervened with his usual flair. No one had bothered Monello after that. Years went by, and he and Michael met only when their schedules allowed. But they broke contact soon after.

Monello, unbeknownst to Michael, had spiraled into an addiction curve as he grew doing drugs and whatnot, and Tommy Giovanni had finally found a way to crush Michael to the core by reaching out to a rather eager Patrick Monello and sell to him. If only Michael had known what demons were troubling his little friend, he would not have let him succumb to them.

Michael had found him in his home, the image of his body lying on the floor... Monello had OD-ed. At *Sixteen.*

Michael still dreamt of Patrick.

He went back to his spot by the window. Settling in and gazing back at the crowd, he saw it; a Mercedes had arrived at the spot he was expecting it to. The crowd had erupted into applause and adulation.

Such fools, thought Michael.

As if on cue, he stepped out of the car. A security guard came and held ajar the door to his car and out of his way. A boot landed on the ground; polished, expensive. Seconds later, out came Michael's target. He was, within the next ensuing seconds, surrounded by a swarm of more guards. The walls of human flesh these people hid behind always disgusted Michael. He never went out with any guards; his life was broadcasted on TV and the media as Michael Osborne of Osborne investments all the time, yet he never had any guards. Michael was a master at disguise; he had to become one. No one could tell it was Michael Osborne frequenting the local bar in any of his "looks."

From mafia-born thug to successful businessman and celebrity, Michael thought and laughed.

As per his calculations, he had about thirty seconds to lock his target before he disappeared inside Weston's entrance. That's right; he was coming inside. Michael had carefully chosen his location. While some might say it was the most obvious spot to hide in and the most stupid, he had run calculations, and no law enforcement agency would even think about scaling Weston, especially from the point where he was in. It would take only the best of the best—his equivalent, to figure out his ploy.

He was walking away towards the entrance. Cameras flashed, paparazzi and reporters alike trying to get him to talk; his guards never let him stop. The public and all the press were paved away from the entrance path, held back by carpet poles.

Michael readied his aim, not letting his target out of his mark. Exhaling one last time, he pulled the trigger.

***

The five o'clock news shook up the country.

Parvati was in the shower when her phone pinged. A hand emerged from the drawn shower curtains; she tried to grab her phone. She was one of those productivity hacks people who had a gadget or a system for everything they did to do it faster and efficiently, which was why her phone was neatly placed in a plastic cover with a lanyard that hung from a hooks plate screwed in the wall. She quickly unlocked her phone, a black iPhone 12 with a matte black cover, and sifted through her notifications.

ELLA GRODETSKY HAS TAGGED YOU IN A PHOTO.

RUPERT JAMES COMMENTED ON A PHOTO YOU ARE TAGGED IN.

EMMA BLAKE COMMENTED ON A PHOTO YOU ARE TAGGED IN.

It was annoying as hell for Parvati. Social media was not for her despite what her friends thought of her perfect face-cut, coffee brown skin, heart-shaped lips, a nose that was "to die for," and her beautiful, auburn hair. Ella Grodetsky kept tagging her in group photos (and not other on her single-file shots, anymore, for Parvati had called her out on that) so her Hollywood contacts could get a whiff for her friend. She was a talent booker in Hollywood, always looking around for new faces.

"You are meant to be a star!" She had once told her, trying to get her to meet up with a client of hers. If only Parvati had not been sorority sisters with Grodetsky... She and Ella were best friends. But still. The woman could be quite controlling—and calling her "controlling" was simply being kind.

10

Parvati Bedi worked for the FBI, a fact she had to remind Ella of constantly. She had no time for striking poses and acting.

There was one notification Parvati didn't slide away. It was a text.

CHECKED THE NEWS? THIS IS GOING 2 BE US.
RECEIVED: 5:13 PM

It was from Johnny Whitehill, her partner.

Five minutes later, Parvati was in her living room; her bathrobe neatly packed around her, her hair tied up in a towel turban-ed atop her head. She picked up the remote off its stand in the wall and turned her TV on. It was a 65" smart TV, which doubled as her local cable entertainment as well. FOX was already running a full-fledged feature on the assassination.

"Senator Dudley's early demise is a tragedy for the country. Local police and authorities

11

are yet to..." The news reporter went on with her delivery. They occasionally flashed an image or a two or some footage of the assassination. Nothing too gory. But only because this was a political assassination. Had it been anything blue-collar and her screen would have been a flurry of images and "well-detailed" footage. "*But it is evident that this assassination attempt, one that the senator's security detail failed to prevent*—" Parvati hit mute, leaving the reporter to carry on the incessant movement of her lips.

The media was at its old tricks again, making mountains out of molehills. What they *should* be reporting, Bedi thought, were the ill-thought-out, *very* public campaigns of the late senator against the Giovanni mafia. The old geezer had practically called open season on himself. Yet, the media was blaming the authorities and the senator's security staff— which was sanctioned by the FBI, by the way.

She was impressed, though. She was sorry for the senator, of course. But for someone to have found an angle *into* an FBI-protected gathering… Mafia-linked assassins were nowhere near this intelligence and evasion.

The senator had reached out and asked for protection following a fourth death threat he had received; a letter with blood on it. While threat number one and two had only been phone calls, threat number three had been an extremely inappropriate prank text. Calling the sender's bluff, the senator had chosen not to *"post nudes" of himself* on his Facebook profile, which had resulted in the bloodied letter.

And now this.

Parvati sent Johnny a text.

CALL ME. SENT: 5:23 PM

Parvati was hungry. She went to her fridge and took note of what was in there. Pizza leftovers from last night, some spaghetti she had cooked up for lunch yesterday but had not got the time to eat, a six-pack of diet

Pepsi—Parvati had a strict diet—and her refrigerated usual. She decided on the pizza and took out a can off the six-pack—to hell with her diet—closing the door on her way back to the dining room.

It was a luxury apartment Parvati was currently settled in. Nothing but the best for the FBI's best, or at least that was how she remembered Ella putting it. She actually missed her old life when there wasn't a care in the world, and all she, Ella, and the rest of their girls had to do was party, get drunk, have fun.

She couldn't get the assassination out of her head, though.

Who was it? How had they done it? Definitely not mafia. They must be ex-military—or FBI, even. But the latter was not possible, for they would have been running tabs from the very beginning. Whoever it was, they were good.

With her pizza only halfway to her mouth, Parvati's phone began to ring.

It was Johnny.

She put it down on her plate and answered.

"Yo, Bedi, what's up?" said Johnny in his usual perfunctory ice-breaker. He always called her by her surname.

"I saw the news." She began.

"And you want in." Johnny hinted at her reply.

"Oh, I do, but we first need to—"

"We are in. Already. Case got assigned to us." Johnny interrupted Parvati again. He did that all the time, even when they were *not* on the phone. Parvati never let that derail her. She was far too composed and mature to let Johnny not-so-English's narcissism get to her.

"Good. Good…" Parvati was satisfied. She wanted this case. She wanted to hunt this master assassin down. No one worked their way through the FBI's security protocols and got away with it. No one ever worked their way through the FBI's anything—period.

"You ready?" Johnny asked Parvati from the other side.

"You bet," Parvati replied.

As if to oblige the blood rush surging through Parvati's veins, something he no doubt must have sensed from her reaction, he said: "Good. Let's get this fucker."

Chapter Two

Morano

Then

It was three of them; three. Michael saw from the other side of the street.

"I've gotta' go," Patricia tried to maneuver her way out of the ambush. Tommy Giovanni blocked her exit, slamming a hand into the wall of the walkway she had been walking on. Bristling, she took a step back where one of Tommy's bullies was already waiting. She walked into him, and he grabbed her from both the sides, pinning her into place.

"HEY!" Michael bellowed from across the street, crossing it in what felt like the speediest five seconds of his life. He walked, a rather daunting walk, the rest of the way to Tommy Giovanni.

"Let her go." Michael felt no other emotion than seething, blinding rage as the words came out of his mouth.

Tommy Giovanni came into his full view. His garb was his usual, green zipper jacket that zipped up to the top torso, the arms of the jacket showing off his biceps; black skinny-jeans that held to his thighs and back snugly. Brown leather boots laced up tightly. Hair gel held his jet-black hair in place. As for his face, it was the same vicious and menacing ever since Michael had known him.

"Or what, Morano?" He snapped back at Michael, chin raised. He was ready for a fight. He was always ready for a fight. His goons left Patricia alone and came to stand next to him. Good. He wanted them as far away from Patricia as possible.

Michael stood his ground, uttering not a word. He wasn't scared of Tommy and his assists; Michael had always held his own in a fight, be it with one or more. But Tommy Giovanni was, well, a Giovanni; the Morano's sworn enemies. He did not want to be the one to start this fight. And so, Tommy swung first. Michael had no choice but to fight.

It was rough.

After about eight minutes, Tommy's "assists" had abandoned the fight, not really having assisted him. Michael had taken only a few punches and kicks but had ultimately sent them running. As for Tommy, well... he never fought alone and only skirted around the idea of leaving himself so that it wouldn't feel like or come across as giving up to his opponent when he actually did both.

"Would love to beat your ass, Morano, but I got things to do. Have fun with your new girlfriend." Having said his farewell taunt, Tommy Giovanni left as quick as lightning. With him gone, Michael turned to Patricia. She was still in shock and utterly embarrassed, gathering her bearings and fussing with her clothes and hair. He wasn't getting any thank you from this one, he deduced after what he did get from her was *a look of contempt. Maybe it was time Michael quit following her to her house every time from school. Both Tommy and Michael were from mafia families, and he guessed boys like him were all the same to a girl like Patricia.*

Michael only nodded to her and turned to leave.

"Wait!" Patricia called out to him, stopping him in his tracks. "Thank you..." she said.

"No problem, Tommy is an ass anyway," Michael responded, trying to lighten the mood. Patricia let loose an unwilling laugh at that. What do you know! It worked.

"That he is... listen. I was heading to the coffee house after dropping my things at my place. Care to join?" Patricia offered.

"Sure," said Michael.

OSBORNE

NOW

"It is done," Michael said into his phone.

"Hmm. Saw the news." It was Luca Giovanni.

"I need to talk to Patricia and my daughter." Michael reminded him.

"Not yet," Luca said slyly, playing with him a bit more.

Michael was infuriated. Some of his old anger back from his old life was trying to push its way through. Michael did everything he could mentally to keep it from returning. His was a fiery rage, all-consuming. Even when he was still Michael Morano, he had an impulse control his contemporaries admired. But when he reached his limit...

He set everything ablaze.

"We had a deal," Michael said level-headedly. There was no messing around with Luca Giovanni. In this case, the apple *had* fallen far from the tree.

"Yeah, well. I changed my mind." Luca replied. Michael could imagine the sly smirk plastered across the bastard's face. But there was nothing he could do. Unless he somehow knew how to bring the dead back to life.

Michael did not rebut Luca and waited for him to respond.

"That is exactly what I want from you, Michael Morano," Luca said, having sensed Michael's unwilling silence. "Absolute submission. I call the shots now, and you're nothing but my little bitch." Luca was goading him. The *prick* and his nerve! Michael had to keep it reeled in. Even a sliver of anger and he would kill them.

"Transfer ten million dollars into an account. Details will be sent on your phone. Fail to make the transaction and I will not only change my mind on keeping your lover and bastard alive but also kill you in ways you couldn't even begin to think of, boy."

Damn...

"After all, it is only fair. A life for a life..." Giovanni was reigning in on his own anger. Such was what ran in the blood of these families. Anger. Pain. An unquenchable thirst for retribution. "Instead, I will make your every day living hell. Make you pay for Tommy's murder."

And just like that, he hung up.

Fresh worry circulated through Michael's veins after processing how Luca had threatened him. He waited for the account details to show up on his phone. Seconds later, he received a text.

RECEIVED: 7:47 PM

After Senator Dudley, Michael could only imagine what heinous crime Giovanni would have him do next. The peace Michael had worked so hard to achieve these last two years, the washing away of his sinful past life; it was all for nothing. While it had been blood and being born in a mafia family that had made a monster out of him, Luca Giovanni was selling his soul to the devil, and there was nothing Michael could do to stop him.

Blood to people like them meant everything. It was a fair yet too high a price to pay for what Michael had done.

A life for a life. Or three, if Michael screwed up.

BEDI

They were damn good at their jobs.

Parvati put her phone on the table in the living room as she stepped a little in the middle for a better view. After only a few minutes at the crime site, she and Johnny had figured out the point of the bullet's origin. The local authorities had ruled Weston out as any apartment in the Hotel would have been a bad vantage point for the shooting. The killer had banked on this and shot from the apartment her partner Johnny Whitehill and she had entered.

Smart. Too smart. Parvati suspected foul play.

"I'll look for prints," Johnny said, his voice distant as he had bothered to talk only when he was almost out of the living room. Parvati highly doubted he would find any. If this hitman was smart enough to outsmart the authorities in the most daringly creative way ever, he was no fool and wouldn't have left any trace of prints.

Parvati started her own search of the apartment.

One thing was certain. The shooter had been hired by someone high profile for this luxury apartment was too lavish for a temporary job. It was also another way to sway the authorities in the wrong direction. While it meant the senator's competition had more to do with the murder—for only someone higher up enough could afford an apartment for their assassin at the Weston—it also meant that whoever had wanted the senator dead could as easily been someone "from the other side of town."

She needed evidence, though, to support her mafia theory.

Going in room after room, Parvati reminisced.

She had been "shy." Most of the field superiors had been doubtful of her placement in the field division. They had fully acknowledged her set of skills, though, both physical and mental—had even gone so far as to say she was the best. Which she was. But they thought someone like her wasn't meant for the field. Parvati had had quite the time trying to figure out what *shy* meant in her superiors' dictionaries, for she was anything but. It had turned out that the shyness they had been referring to was something they believed she was carrying because of her ethnicity.

At the FBI, you were required to do undercover work. This meant you could be, at times, given roles you were not comfortable with.

Parvati had tooth-and-nail-proved to them that she was the best field agent they could wish for. This determination and her performance had warranted a promotion, an even higher pay, and some perks.

Unfortunately, the promotion had also meant that she be teamed up with Johnny Whitehill, an agent almost half of the senior recruits avoided, and *all* of the newbies hated.

Parvati finally came across a door that interested her. For starters, it was the only one that was locked. No problem. She kicked the door open with too much ease. "What the hell…" she trailed off.

The room was wide enough for a person to sit in. For sure. But only so. While the sides were plain, bare walls, the opposing section was nothing but glass. Hundreds of squares of glass, divided by wooden panels. Weird.

Good; she was looking for weird. She decided to do a sweep before calling in Whitehill; the prick would only try to make it unbearable for her.

The sweep was pretty easy: there was *nothing* in there *to* sweep. The room had no furniture and was empty.

Parvati started to look for prints. There were too many glasses, and she started from the ones at the bottom of the glass wall. One, then two. Three, four... On and one she went.

When she saw it, though, she knew there was no mistaking it.

Traces of purple powder lined the floor at the far end of the room. She would have missed it had it not been for her flashlight; fingerprints were a tricky business, and yet she had found something even better.

It was gunshot residue.

Normally, gunshot residue was too insignificant to be noticed like this. Parvati could think of only one assault rifle capable of leaving residue both of this color and amount. The purple color was from the coating that came after the bullet was dipped in a particular poison. The coroner's report was yet to be released. Parvati made a mental note to look into it and see whether any traces of the purple poison used on the bullet fired were in the senator's blood.

While the assault rifle was super rare, so was the arms broker that dealt it. Not the dealer, to be exact. But your *chances of finding* said dealer were. If you were not an intended customer, you would never know where to look.

Parvati, however, knew exactly where to find her.

Chapter Three

OSBORNE

NOW

Michael stood viewing the city; it lay across so minuscule from up above his office. The glass windows refracted the sun pouring sunlight, the glare missing his face by only a few inches. The sunlight that penetrated his pent-house office never could reach past his neck when he stood in an exact spot; the spot where he was standing.

The view always calmed Michael.

It was disturbing, really, to think that a man could find solace—peace, even—after murdering someone in cold blood. But then again, this wasn't intended murder. But wasn't it? Even back when he was a Morano, Michael had had a number of fights; some were more bloodier than the others. It had never come to the point of bloodshed. Or at least until that day...

Reeling back his emotions and with them a breath, Michael exhaled, calmly letting the past slip through the stensile roots that were his connection to the Morano mafia. The water slipped past; the roots were left dry. It was only a matter of time before Luca Giovanni lit them up with his dark flames—

"Mikey! Hey!" Jeanette walked into his office, uninvited as usual.

"Jean, hello…" Michael tried to make conversation. Honestly, he would take Jeanette and her incessant gibberish over thoughts of Luca Giovanni any day.

"I am sensing… distress," she said as she walked her way to him in heels that were highly inappropriate for a mother of two one-year-olds. Jeanette had had twins last year, something she never paused to remind the world about. "There is so much pain. A lot of pain, oh!" The woman had the balls— or whatever was *Jeanette's* equivalent of balls—to tug at Michael's teal tie. His hands were in the side pockets of his slim-cut dress pants, and the only thing he could do was raise an eyebrow at her.

"Oh, cheer up!" She said, letting go of his tie. She walked to his table and leaned against it, inspecting her nails. Michael did a once over of his head of marketing. The inappropriate heels went with a business, knee-length skirt too tightly wound around her to classify as business attire, a white ruffled lace blouse neatly tucked from the sides under a pink coat that matched the skirts, and a blonde updo with surprisingly minimum makeup and non-existent jewelry—just pearl earrings, really.

"How's your mother, Jean?" Michael remembered to ask. Jeanette's mother had been diagnosed with stage two lymphoma a few weeks back. It had been the talk of the company how Jeanette had not requested for a leave. Michael had offered it himself, but she had refused. "We come from a strong bloodline," she had said. "My mother will fight it and win." Despite what his employees said about Jeanette McCalvin, she was not of a cold heart. In fact, Michael respected the fact that she had been working all the while her mother was in chemo. It had been Mrs. McCalvin's request only that her daughter not be allowed to see her in her condition. Both mother and daughter loved each other; while one wanted to give the other everything, the other didn't want anything out of love.

And this was why Michael endured Jeanette McCalvin wordlessly.

"She is fine. She. Is. Fine." Jeanette's mood had immediately changed after being asked about her mother. She became more conscious all of a sudden. "So, um, I came here to talk about… um, some changes I'd like addressed in how we reach out to our customers. Shall I book a table for two at Kwang's?"

"Why don't you email me—"

"Kwang's it is," Jeanette continued, uninterrupted but interrupting him. "Oh my goodness, look how thin those arms of yours look! You have grown so soft. Tell me you still have your six-packs—"

"Mr. Osborne?" It was Zoey, his assistant. And savior.

"Yes, Zoey. What is it?" Michael was relieved.

"Your 2 o'clock is here; shall I bring them in?" 2 o'clock was Michael and Zoey's code to *get her (Jeanette) out of here* in Michael's case, and *don't worry, I've got her (Jeanette)* in Zoey's case.

"Yes, please," Michael said. He couldn't help but smile a little at how ridiculous the whole affair was. Better a smile than laughter; Jeanette wouldn't let him rest if she heard him so much as a huff. Zoey smiled, too, containing her laughter at the magnanimous pain in the head that was Jeanette McCalvin.

And the head wasn't the only place where Jeanette brought pain.

Literally dragging Jeanette out by her entire arm, Zoey made good work of walking her out, making up excuses for Michael and that he had to work, eventually leading her out of his office.

RING. RING.

34

It was Michael's landline.

RING. RING.

As he walked over to answer it, the dreadful thought of the caller being Luca Giovanni crossed his head. It was not like Giovanni to call him two days in a row. Michael shuddered to think what he would ask of him this time—

"Hello?" It was Corbin, his accounting analyst. Otherwise known as *numbers* among the company circles. Lost in his train of thought, Michael didn't know when he had picked up the phone. Corbin had been waiting patiently, though.

"Hi, Corbin, what can I do for you? Michael said.

"Hey, so, a client just called, and guess what?" He asked Michael, whose panicking was rising again. Before Michael could formulate and utter a reply, Corbin answered his own question.

"The client wants to buy-in. The client wants to buy-in! A majority stock with ten million dollars." Corbin finished.

"That's good news..." Michael was confused.

"Yeah, it is! And in our disaster relief subsidiary. No one even touches it. What an outcome!" Next, Corbin went on and on about financial backwardness with the subsidiary and what he thought Michael should do.

Transfer ten million dollars into an account...

"Who's the buyer?" Michael asked Corbin.

"Oh, she didn't say. Just a happy, opportunistic investor." *She*?

"So, boss, I've got work to do. Did you want something?"

"Nothing you can help with, I'm afraid. Thanks, Corbin." Michael hung up.

Just then, Zoey came back. "Hey, got rid of our little Nancy Drew situation; how's everything on your end?" she asked.

"Just got interesting," Michael said, head and heart in two different dimensions.

"Great, have fun! I'll be right outside." She closed the doors, and all was silent again, just like it had been when Michael had stood city-gazing.

He didn't believe in coincidence, Michael reminded himself. He had to find out who this mystery investor was before it was too late.

BEDI

Johnny stopped the car outside of the abandoned pathway leading to the abandoned cottage in the city woods Parvati had asked him to drive to. Parvati was a sound driver herself—everybody on the FBI's roster knew how to, in fact, it was Parvati who usually drove them. She let him because she had to focus on their mission.

Anna Solonik was a tough old bird. Getting her to divulge details of the her buyer would be tricky. Throughout her career, Parvati had learned that while force and determination ultimately had people talking, some knew how to evade capture fearing the very torture in store for them, while the rest—and a very rare few—never spoke.

Solonik would talk, Parvati reassured herself. She would make her talk. Besides, they had no other leads and Parvati *had* to find this assassin.

Johnny got out of the car and Parvati followed. Her phone pinged and she ignored it. There was no sign of animal life around, let alone the dealer. But then again, she "let herself be found" to only her intended customers. Parvati had been an intended customer, once (a story for another time), which is how she knew about this off-radar cottage.

Knock. Knock knock. Tap. Knock. Tap tap. Knock. Parvati did the secret knock she had been told to do when she had been her customer. The old widow gave a new knock to each customer; Parvati just hoped that the one she had received long, long ago would trigger some semblance of recoginition.

No answer.

Parvati tried again. Still, nothing.

"Let's try my way." Johnny said not less than five seconds after the dead silence following Parvati's knocking. He inhaled an unnecessarily deep breath, the kicked the wooden door to the cottage down. The idiot. If Solonik had any doubts about running away, that also if she *was,* in fact, here, Johnny's kick and the slamming door must have had them scattered away for good. They wanted compliance; not evasion.

They entered, guns poised. While Solonik was an arms dealer, she previously had ties to the Russian mafia and knew her way with guns in more ways than one.

The had entered her living room, she figured. There was a lone sofa in the middle facing the TV on the far end. Some photographs lined the walls, all fake. Solonik was in none of them. Beside the sofa was a small table upon which lay a half eaten sandwich and a cup of coffee.

"Still warm," said Johnny, pick it up an inspecting it.

Solonik was here.

BLAM!

A bullet fired its way missing Johnny's ear and into the wall. They both ducked, readying for action. Solonik had a shotgun and they were in close quarters. This shouldn't be as difficult as Parvati had been expecting it to be.

BLAM! BLAM! BLAM!

The woman had gone mad.

"Hold it down, Solonik! We have you surrounded!" Parvati tried to get her to surrender.

"I'm no fool, you ungrateful bitch!" Came Anna's reply. Johnny couldn't help but laugh which Parvati ignored. "Had you brought an armada, I would have known hours ago!" Johnny then looked at Parvati, perplexed. She didn't reciprocate his perplexity. They had to get to her.

Parvati motioned to Johnny with two fingers and a fist. That meant "I have a vantage point, be my decoy so I can pinpoint her location." Johnny complied, for once, as Parvati tried to get Anna to talk.

"I will kill you, Solonik! If you want to live, tell me who bought the Poison Lavendar and a shotgun from you." Parvati said, still crouched in her position.

"You think I am going to *talk* to you after you come barging in like—"

BLAM, Anna fired as Johnny tried to derail her. She had missed, of course. It had been enough to get Anna inside the living room where Parvati was ready to take her down . She got up from her crouch and shot a bullet at her shooting arm. Anna dropped the shotgun from her hand, using the other to grab on to the bullet wound.

This was all Johnny needed to pin Solonik down. He landed on top of her as she cried out in pain. "Get off me, bastard!" She spat in Johnny's mouth. It was high and mighty of him to stay as he was, saying nothing back to the bulbous woman.

"Tell. Me. Now. Who bought from you?" Parvati said, standing over Johnny who still had her pinned down.

"I am telling you shit!" She retorted a comeback. Honestly, this woman...

Parvati had no choice but to at first gently pin her bleeding arm with her boot, then increase pressure to get her to talk. She kept quiet, moaning only to the pain reverberating through her arm. Parvati put a little bit of additional pressure and that made her shout.

"Was it a Giovanni? Was it anyone from that family?" Parvati asked. Johnny looked up at her with his not-again-with-the-mafia-conspiracy look. She ignored him. Nothing. Parvati pressed her arm again and Anna shouted, a few tears rolling down the side of her eyes on the ground.

"MORANO! It was a Morano! Anna finally surrendered.

"Morano?" Parvati said looking at Johnny. "But how's that possible? All the Morano heirs are dead. That family has run no operations ever since… ever since Tommy Giovanni." Parvati couldn't believe it. Solonik had always been a liar, protecting the identities of her most lucrative clients.

"One still lives," she said. She was in pain; they both could see. Johnny eased up a bit of his weight, giving her room.

"Who? Who still lives?" Parvati asked.

The first thing you were taught when you joined ranks with the FBI was: never let your guard down. They did extensive training on you in a way you would never be able to forget. It was surprising how most of the agents always did let it down not in the situations they are trained for, but completely unrelated others.

Before Parvati could say anything else, Anna Solonik took advantage of Johnny's having lifted himself off her and from the front pocket of her flannel, took out a pill that she threw into her mouth, gulping it before either Johnny or Parvati could register.

Johnny tried to get her to spit, but Parvati knew it was too late. Minutes later, Solonik was foaming from her mouth.

Cyanide, Parvati registered, disappointed.

Chapter Four

MORANO

THEN

His captor finally removed the sack from head, allowing him to breathe.

The view of a room suddenly appeared. It was someone's... study? It sure looked like it. Michael Osborne whirred his head around, frantically, trying to figure out where he was. Then his captor finally came from beind him, taking the seat across from him. Michael realized his hands had been untied, but not before he realized who his captor was.

"How did you find me?" Michael demanded. Richie had had the gall to kidnap him and had brought him to God only knew where.

"Giovanni wants blood for blood." Richie told him.

"What do you mean?" Michael asked him.

"He wants us all *for the murder you committed 8 years ago." Richie said. Michael could not believe it.*

"Where is Loution?" Michael wanted to deal with the Blood Lord's leader for this and not

some young cub to have joined the pack upon his mother's unending requests.

"Dead." Richie put it just like that. "they are all dead," He added, putting some papers on the table. Michael took a look. They were newspaper clippings of weird, inexplicable accidents. "And I am next," Richie said after letting Michael thoroughly look through the clippings. Boy dies in car accident. Brothers murdered by men of "unknown origin." Man shot dead while hiking. Man accidentally dies of electrocution when relaxing in his pool. Boy run down by car; dies on the spot. Customer poisoned in local tea house...

John, Matt, Rob, Paul, Eddie, Joey, Loution. They were his cousins. They were his brothers. He had led them to their deaths.

"You gotta' help me, man. He will kill me. Come back to New York. Come back to the family." Richie pleaded. Going back to the Morano family was not a possibility. Michael had put too much between his past and his

present and he would not let himself be taken by his darkness again...

Michael nodded his head no. "I can't."

"You killed his kid. There is blood on your hands of not only Tommy Giovanni but your brothers, too." Richie said. "You were the first born of Frederick Giovanni and we all believed you to be our true leader than Loution. The Blood Lords took your every word as gospel. And what did you lead us toward? Ruin! For a crime that you committed."

Michael was rendered speechless.

"When he comes for me and kills me, my blood will also be on your hands."

Richie Morano was killed the very next day.

***

A day after Richie's death, Michael's phone rang and he answered.

"Who is this?" Michael asked. It was an unknown number and this never happened to him. He had been very careful about it when he had switched his identity after leaving his past life. And anybody who called him was somebody, not nobody.

"Michael? Michael Morano?" It was a woman.

"I am sorry. This is not him." Michael was already on the defensive.

"Michael... this is Patricia Grey. I... I had the baby." Said Patricia. While these ten years of his life had made other things seem age a twenty, Micahel could never forget Patricia, his first love. Michael remembered Patricia. They had dated for a while back when Michael was still a Morano. He did not need to even ask her, but she told him anyway.

"Your daughter is in grave dan—" Patricia was cut and a man took over.

"If you want to see your daughter alive, you will do exactly as I tell you, Morano."

The man hung up. It had been Luca Giovanni, Tommy's father and head of the Giovanni family.

OSBORNE

NOW

It was hard not to think of how Michael had got where he was. All his sins and his past; sometimes, they just came back in such an unrelenting way that even his resolve failed to deter them. Michael stood at the door of Ahmed Assef's house, then man who Michael had able to determine had bought in for the ten mills from yesterday. Disaster relief was the kind of investment only a few opted to invest in. No natural calamity occurred in this part of the states.

His disaster relief firm did help hundreds in times of, well, man-made calamities.

He had to know who this Assef was and if he was in any way connected to Luca Giovanni and his… plans for him and his family. So far, his knocking had brought not so much as a grunt from the resident inside.

"Hello? Mr. Assef?" Michael said, not letting his frustration claw its way out. It would have to get in line behind the *other things* currently trying to claw their way out of his head. To his surprise, he heard footsteps closing in. Then came the voice of a woman.

"Salam Alaikum?" She said.

Michael had muslim employees and had had enough of chats with them at parties and business meetings to know what that perfunctory, greeting phrase meant. "Peace be upon you, too. I gather you are Mrs. Assef? May I speak to him, please?" Michael said, all kindness and courtesy.

"I am sorry. My English not good. Assef not home. I not per..." Mrs. Assef flatlined, trying to complete her sentence. "No—no permission to see outside men." She finished. The struggle had been something to contend with, thought Michael. More for him than he bet for poor Mrs. Assef. From the sound of her voice, she seemed to Michael in her early thirties. He knew muslims to be a bit conservative, with antiquated practices. He had also known muslims who were quite modern—the kind that worked at his company.

"It is alright, Mrs. Assef. Please, let him know Mr. Osborne visited and would like a word." Michael said, hushing his voice up a little at "Mr. Osborne." Even as Michael Osborne, he wore disguises for his new hair was still not enough to paint over Michael Morano, his past self.

"I am sorry, I not hear what you say." Mrs. Assef said from behind her door.

Jee. Zus.

Michael took out his business card from his wallet and wrote a small message on the back with a ballpoint pen he always had on him. "Give him this note I am leaving on your doorstep," he told her, leaving his card on the Assef's doormat. When a safe distance, away, Michael turned to look. Sure enough, a scarf-clad woman came out, picked up his card and went back inside.

This Assef guy was as legit as legitimacy itself could get.

***

Michael never took his car service when he wanted to go incognito. In fact, his get up right now included a ridiculously long denim jacket worn over an off-white hoodie. He wore white sneakers, like the kids today wore, with skinny jeans that complimented his look. Zoey, his secretary, took care of his wardrobe. Even his go-incognito look. The beanie, though, that he wore was of his own volition. A fringe of his hair had escaped and partially covered an eye but all of his forhead. Whatever he wore, though, he filled out his clothes.

Gyming provided a good distraction.

He would take a subway down to a café he frequented, then contact a trusted driver who take him home. When next he came on another one of his incognito missions, he would have different route planned out. While it was exhausting, security was important. While he was doing everything he could to save Patricia and his daughter, a daughter whose name even he did not know, he had people after him, too.

And not just paparazzi that had been gunning for him ever since he had cracked the Forbes' 30 Men Under 30.

Michael stumbled into a woman, such had been the thicket of his thoughts. He apologized immediately. The woman didn't utter a word. Her gaze was so intent on the building on their left that even Michael could not help but look. It was Richmond High, the school Michael himself had gone to. He was amazed at happening upon his old high school like this. It was… weird coincidence.

"Ma'am, are you alright?" He asked the lady, who finally turned to look at him. It took a her a second to register any emotion. But she did, it was of pure disgust and horror. Before Michael got a chance to say anything, he knew what followed was not going to be good.

"I know you… I KNOW YOU!" Her voice rose from flimsy whisper to loud anger.

"I am sorry, I—" She cut Michael off.

"Michael Morano! You are Michael Morano!" The lady was practically screeching now.

Michael felt like being hit with a hundred needles. He was simpy speechless.

"You had my little boy killed! You had him killed!" said the lady; a frenzy of emotion and pointing fingers. Michael was finally brought back to his senses and he immediately whirled around to check for passerby. They were alone, but it felt like being accused of murder in a courtroom full of people.

Michael's gaze, in his frenzy of looking around, ended up at Richmond High's architecture. It struck him right then.

Patrick Monello had gone to Richmond High, too.

Michael ran away from Patrick's mother, his eyes welling up with tears, as she kept shouting away at him in the distance.

THE ASSISSAN

When he had begun whirring his head around, he was sure he would see him hidden away. But, he guessed, the kid's mother and the school—the school, he laughed—must have been too pungent reminders of the kid's death for anything else to make sense to his target.

The woman and her screaming had been all that he had needed. Following the suspect had not been a wasite of time. The mother's sudden loss of impulse control had led him to confirm his suspicions.

When he had first been assigned the assignment, he had been hesitant. *Are they all not dead?* He had asked his commissioner. *We want to find out*, he had been told. It had been days of research and of espionage ever since. He didn't mind, of course. With each passing day had come generous amounts of money transferred to his account.

The Morano boys had formed a group of sorts; The Blood Lords, they had called themselves back in the day. Badasses whom no one should mess with. It was a part of growing up as a man in any mafia family, or so his commissioner had told him. Micahel's Having run away had given his commissioner, Enzo Morano, brother to the deceased Frederick Morano and former Mafia head, complete reign over the family and its reserves and the undying loyalty and support of the remaining elders of the family: Christina, Esposito, and Helga Morano. He was the new family head with Michael gone. And Michael, he had confirmed, had led his cousins, the sons of the Morano elders, to their deaths having involved them in his fight with the Giovanni mafia and its own heir.

Previously believed to be dead by both himself and his family, the very dapper-styled guy he had been following walking an usual route to an unusual home in the suburbs was indeed Michael Morano; the Last Blood Lord. Alive and well.

But not for long. For the Morano family wanted him dead.

Blood for blood.

Chapter Five

OSBORNE

NOW

By this point in Michael's life, he was pretty sure nothing would be able to unsettle him. The bloodied letter he had found delivered to him last night was rather disturbing. Whose blood was it? When Michael saw the all-too-familiar cursive, though, the blood become the least of his problems.

BLOOD FOR BLOOD...

It was Enzo Morano, his uncle.

Readying himself for the guest speaker session he had been invited to at NYU by some students, the letter was all Michael could think about next morning. His family had found him, it seemed. And they wanted revenge for how Michael had gotten their sons, his cousins—the Blood Lords, killed at the hands of Luca Giovanni for a murder he had committed.

Michael relied on his calm to get him through. He picked up his phone and text-messaged his car service to cancel. He wanted to drive himself, for a change. It would help clear his head.

Taking one last look in the mirror, something he found doing absolutely ridiculous but had been forced into doing by his God-bless-her assistant, he determined himself "ready" for the occasion. Grabbing his keys and wallet, Michael Osborne left for NYU for delivery of his speech to young, budding entrepreneurs.

As if they would ever be able to understand how Michael had got to where he was.

Driving did help his mind escape from the all the horrors that letter had brought back.

Like all the people, cars, trees, and shops passing by, his memories were becoming a messy blur. Michael had left the windows to both the sides open, letting in fresh air. It was that or the bone-chilling air conditioner of his car. The weather wasn't that intense to warrant use of air conditioning. Michael still had to make sure that by the time he arrived at NYU, he wasn't sweaty.

The world had changed, Michael observed. It was… evolving? Yes. People had evolved. Yet, his family was still stuck in the past not letting go of their mafia ways. It was another reason, Michael had later realized becoming an Osborne, that would have eventually separated him from his family had Tommy Giovanni not brought about his own end.

Also, Patrick would still be alive…

Michael hit the brakes instinctively, his car skidding to a halt in time for the girl to make running to the other side.

"Watch where you're going, asshole!" She said, raising a hand, and a very specific finger with it, gracing him with the most honorable gesture man-kind had invented. Turning around, she disappeared around the corner. Good, she hadn't recognized him. It was weird, really. No paparazzi had ambushed him. He was in his complete, Michael-Osborne-of-Osborne-Investments garb.

Some days were easier, he guessed.

A smile escaped through all the remaining tension, spreading across his face, and Michael reveled in it. Screw his family. Screw Giovanni (who had been awfully quiet ever since the transfer). Michael would enjoy his time at NYU. Heck, he would even let some of the students take pictures with him, something he was strictly against. The lesser the media coverage, the lesser the chances were of his facing popping up under someone undesirable's eyes and him being recognized. For a different shade of hair could only go so far keeping one indistinguishable.

He was going to enjoy himself today, something he hadn't allowed himself to do all this time for the horrors of his past had kept him from it.

Little did Michael know of the very much tangible horror that was following him completely undetected.

THE ASSASSIN

It was surprising how an urban assault vehicle could pass for a normal jeep among these streets. People really didn't think much of the worst that could happen. Then again, Terrorism didn't run as amuck as it did in some of the other countries he had worked in.

But then again, all of on-vehicle arsenal was hidden from view until he activated his machine gun and mini-missile launchers.

Michael Morano, it seemed, was perfectly ignorant of his pursuit. He made sure, though, that he didn't drive up too close to his car. Enzo Morano had trained him on all things Michael Morano. His nephew was smart, cunning, intelligent. There was no fooling him. By his calculations, though, anybody the kind of smart Michael was according to his uncle *should* have been able to detect even a well-disguised assault jeep following them.

Maybe he wasn't as good as his uncle claimed. Or maybe it was private life that had made him go soft over the years. It had been only two, he had been told.

The assassin was enjoying this assignment.

As if suddenly having received some sort of permission, he undid the disguise on his vehicle. Jeep moving, he stood up and brought from the back his machine gun, adjusting it to the notches that awaited it on his bonnet. Next, he did something that gave him the high he needed before a kill.

He lit up a cigarette.

OSBORNE

Crackling machine gun bullets pulled a too-happy Michael out of his reverie.

He swerved his car out of the way of the onslaught. The bullets went flying God knows where. Michael heard screaming in the distance. Hopefully it was just terrified civilians and no one had been hurt.

The Michael Morano inside him, whom he was surprised to discover still alive, told him realistically that *people had died already*.

Michael brought himself back to the situation. He had to be careful so as to not get anybody else hurt. It was a new low for his family to hit; hiring a hitman to dispose of their nephew. The letter... Enzo must have had this hitman deliver it to him. He wouldn't risk coming all the way to New York just deliver a threat.

"Fuck," said Michael.

He drove as fast as he could. He was going in another direction and away from NYU that wasn't that far away from where he had been ambushed. He had to protect those children at all costs.

Time to assess his enemy, Michael thought.

While the bullets' barrage had ended, his attacker was still pursuing him. He was trying to observe his assault jeep—it was an assault jeep, a kind of urban assault vehicle, Michael had been able to guess at least that much—as best as he could from rear view. The bastard had a cigarette in his mouth, which he had not soon after Michael had begun trying to get a sense of his face, spat out of his mouth and covered the remainder of his face with a slip-on mask from down his neck. There was nothing now but a black face belonging to a black-clad figure speeding what had to be the biggest jeep Michael had ever seen towards him.

"Son of a—"

BOOOOOM!

The small missile that flew out and away from the jeep that Michael had been lucky enough to see before it was too late and spin his car elsewhere, went blasting into a clothing store he sped past seconds before impact. There were screams and terrified people in the back and there was nothing Michael could do to help them.

He had to lead him away from these people...

The NYC High Bridge had been closed for construction, it occurred to Michael. He suddenly knew how he would deal with his attacker.

THE ASSISSAN

It had been nearly an hour but Michael Morano was leading him someplace else instead of NYU. Social media helped with espionage, thought the assassin. He knew Michael was going to NYU for his little speech a day ago and had hence decided to make an appearance. He had to hand it to the kid; he had some great driving skills. No one would have lasted this long.

Perhaps Enzo had been right about Michael. He was his nephew after all. What he wouldn't do to see the kid in face-to-face combat. His instructions had been clear: bring his head. And that is exactly what he was going to do.

So, he sped his jeep up even more and went after him over what appeared to be a bridge

OSBORNE

Not such a genius after all, Michael thought.

The assassin had followed him all the way to the bridge. There was water flowing underneath. This was not a local, he determined. For anybody who was from around here would know of the High Bridge closure. There was a wide gap in the center, enough for even a car as speedy as his assassin's to not be able to make to the other side.

And that was Michael's plan.

He began slowing the speed of his car. Not soon after, his attacker let lose a rain of bullets.

"Shit." Michael had brought his car to an immediate stop not too far from the gap. He got out and hid behind. The bullets stopped when the jeep was only a little distance away from his car and the trap that awaited him. Michael could see from he was hidden. His attacker launched himself out of the jeep which came crashing into his car—not before he had ducked far away from the collision.

Both the cars went tumbling down.

His attacker was disoriented from the jump and was still trying to get his bearings.

Michael used this to his advantage and retrieved his gun from the inside of his blazer. He had taken one with him and kept it in his glove compartment. The letter had been a mistake.

Before the assassin could retrieve on of his own weapons, Michael shot the bastard in one leg. He knelt, screaming out in pain. He shot him in the other leg, too.

"Who sent you?" Michael bellowed at him. Nothing. He said nothing. Michael didn't want to kill him. He was a killer no more. Instead, he walked past him back the way they had come.

But before he left him, he kicked him in his stomach, and his injured legs, leaving him to howl in pain.

The news never failed to impress Parvati.

It hadn't taken her long to figure the whole thicket out. Michael Morano was still alive. But had changed his name and identity. It wasn't smart of him, though, to hide in plain sight. That logic didn't work all the time.

Michael Morano was Michael Osborne's past; Michael Osborne was Michael Morano's future.

Meanwhile, toxicology had confirmed presence of the poison Parvati had found. It also meant Michael had killed the senator. Why would he though? Successful, rich businessman of Osborne investments? Because somebody made him. It was only her speculation, but she knew she wasn't wrong about this. Michael Morano had run away from his past and it had caught up to him in the cruelest way possible.

He had set a target on his head the day he had killed Tommy Giovanni, the only son of mafia druglord Luca Giovanni. Her investigation had revealed that Luca had killed all of the Blood Lords in retribution for a crime committed by none of them but Michael Morano. So, not only was Luca Giovanni after Michael, but so were his own family, the Moranos. Whatever plans they had for the last blood lord, and whomever of the two had leverage on him, both families would have to get in line.

Because the last blood lord was hers.

Chapter Six

OSBORNE

Michael was following his attacker from two weeks ago.

It was funny, really, how someone skilled enough had been able to find him yet had no idea he was being followed. If Michael didn't want to be found, no one found him. This assassin was good. No doubt. But not great, apparently, for as he parked his car outside of Everest Mart, so did Michael.

It was time to shop.

Michael went in a little later after him, he was in a wheel chair since Michael had shot him in the legs. He was surprised at his fast recovery. There were security cameras up along God knew how many walls and he had to keep his shocking new appearance— blond fringe and even weirder clothes, garb picked really more out of desperation than anything— from appearing too out-of-the-ordinary. Even when being captured by cam-footage.

He spotted him at aisle three. Whatever would he want from that aisle? Michael went into aisle two: bathroom and beauty. If he didn't know any better, this move actually complimented his get up. A woman was walking her way out, a child prancing about her knees, tried to take his mother's cart in his own little hands. She quickly tugged her child away from Michael upon seeing him.

Great, Michael thought. If truth be told, he wasn't that awkwardly dressed; the situation had called for a look this… distinguished. And he had opted for it. Michael quickly began looking at his target through whatever boxes and store products would allow him to peek. He was, it seemed, picking up cereal boxes.

So, his target had a family. Or was into Cocoa Puffs himself. That would be really weird and fitting at the same time. Michael followed him around. He was shopping for basic, household grocery, something typical of the mother of the house. A single parent, then.

It would hard, then, killing him. Michael didn't want to take a child's parent away.

But he had no choice.

ENZO

Enzo Morano opened the box, and sure enough, his breath was knocked right away.

It contained a severed head. And it wasn't just any head. It was the head of the assassin he had hired. Enzo supposed he saw it coming. But not like this. The message was clear from his nephew; he couldn't have been any more transparent:

STAY AWAY. OR THERE'LL BE MORE.

Frederick had always proven himself to be a man of means; the apple had not fallen that far from the tree. Heck, it had fallen right underneath.

All Enzo had wanted was to avenge his own sons, and those of his siblings. It is what any of them had wanted. It was not fair how Luca Giovanni had murdered their children for a crime they had not directly been a part of. Tommy Giovanni's blood was solely on Michael's hands. Yet he was alive and well.

But their sons were not.

He couldn't have anymore bloodshed. As head of the family, he had to protect what was left of it. He knew exactly what to do. Taking his phone out from the back pocket of his jeans, he sent a group-text to his siblings.

IT IS DONE; MICHAEL IS DEAD.SENT: 7:41 PM

OSBORNE

Michael had been surprised to hear from Luca after so long.

He got into his van, having locked the back up securely. Of course, Giovanni had kept its contents a secret. Michael had opted out of asking him about them, as well. Especially when this was to be *his last chance to save his family*, or so Luca had claimed over the phone. Where this endgame would lead him, he had no idea. But he was quite certain that it wasn't going to lead him to his daughter and Patricia.

He had to protect his family. A family he never knew he had had. The world was cruel like that, Michael thought. It was Patrick first. Then old man Osborne. He would not let Patricia and his daughter be taken away from him. He simply would not. He would do anything to protect them.

Which is why he had, without question, agreed to transport Luca's mysterious package through his mysterious van.

Hanna. His daughter's name was Hanna.

Luca, the bastard, had granted him one call. Patricia had spoken for a minute, then had given the phone to their daughter. While Patricia had not mentioned how old she was, it was clear from speaking to her she was barely nine. A tear, Michael allowed himself to admit later on—despite the wetness of his eyes in that moment—that a tear *had* escaped him, trickling down his cheek upon hearing his daughter talk.

Are you my daddy?

Luca had taken the phone right then, the sick bastard.

Michael drove to the spot Luca had marked with some red flag. Michael wondered how he would be able to see anything in this dark. Parking his car in a corner, he got out in search for this red flag. There was a lighthouse nearby, the only source of light in the darkest night. Soon enough, Michael saw a spot up on pole being lighted by the occasional rounds of the lighthouse beam's light. Sure enough, there was a red flag hoisted up there.

"Are you Mr. Jenkins?" Came someone's voice.

"Yes," Michael said. Mr. Jenkins was to be the name Michael was to use for this operation, Luca had said. He had failed to mentioned that he would actually have to use it.

"Great. Have you got the package with you?" It was a man with an English accent. Michael nodded his yes to which he said: "Well, what are you waiting for? Get in the van? I'll write the address down for ya'."

Michael was too tired to even argue with him. He nodded and then went back inside his car. He was growing tired of these games. Was it merely to annoy him? It appeared so. Michael took from the man the piece of paper he had promised.

Revving the engine to a start, Michael went to this new place to deliver Luca's bloody package.

BEDI

Even when not on duty, Parvati couldn't help but wonder how far she'll be able to get tomorrow when she resumed work on the Osborne case. Whitehill had, of course, dismissed her theory when it lay, black and white, in plain white. Good, Parvati had thought. She wanted him away. Far away, in fact.

The powder. The bullet. Solonik.

Parvati knew the man found screaming at the end of NYC High was connected to this whole affair. Afterall, from the two remains of the busted-up cars that were recovered from the unrelenting waters underneath, one had belonged to Michael Osborne. The vehicle was registered under his name and

Michael had gone to great lengths to conceal that bit of information from the authorities.

The bastard was probably being chased by a deal-gone-bad client equally capable of the atrocities of the mafia. The urban assault vehicle was no ordinary jeep, it was an A grade vehicle, the kind that Parvati often had uncovered from her previous operations into mafia strongholds.

That was what she hated about these families. In settling their private affairs, they didn't dare a glance outside of their vendettas. 13 civilians had been reported killed from the fire of the machine gun. Michael Osborne, Parvati had learned, was to deliver a speech at NYU. Upon carefully inspecting the case, she figured he had changed his route.

He was trying to save as many people as possible...

Still. People had died because of him. She was going to get him.

Parvati entered the gym. It was open, still, and she usually frequented it at this late hour. The attendants present didn't bat an eye or say a word as she got into her routine. Exercise helped her focus. The various motions she had her body do were an incredible way to extract wayward focus and converge into one whole.

She worked up a sweat. Like she always did. It was here that she let out her aggression; it was here that she could focus. This place, probably off the agency's notice and any others, was the secret of her success. Hours spent here would result in the next day being a case-solved day or a promotion (like last time). It was like her luck charm, the kind you never wore but knew did wonders for you.

Parvati had solved each of her cases after a night spent at this gym and while she knew she had already solved this new one, she needed an edge over what was to come her way tomorrow.

Chapter Seven

OSBORNE

It was a terrible, tragic disaster.

Michael was in his boardroom when one of the investors he had called in for a short meeting lit the fire all over his plans for the future. He had stood up, his phone in his hand, eyes not drifting away from the device even as he announced the bombing.

"There's been a bombing. At New Mercy Hospital!" He had finally said.

It had first begun as a flimsy wave of murmurs, but the descent caught up rather quickly. In a matter of seconds, the investors began rising up from their seats and bidding him farewell. Michael hadn't even called the meeting off yet.

Zoey came inside and Michael immediately turned to her.

"What's going on?" He asked, as the last of the investors left the boardroom.

"Sir, New Mercy hospital… there's been a blast there. A big one. They've reported around 37 casualties and 18 people are alive but in critical condition…," Zoey began explaining what exactly had transpired at the hospital. Michael zoned out at the mere mention of the place. Zoey asked Michael if he was alright. Of course, Michael didn't hear. She then turned the TV in the boardroom on and told him she'll be back with a glass of water.

The first channel only was covering the disaster.

"Authorities seemed to have narrowed this one down to a single-file suspect. While we are heartbroken over the attempted murder of innocent people, it does come across as a horrendous shock."

Michael felt an emptiness; nothing but emptiness taking over him, like dark weeds growing from the ground he stood upon, snaking their way around his legs, up till his chest and neck, and finally inside his mouth, choking him from the inside.

Michael got only bits and pieces of what the news reporter was saying.

SLAM. The glass in Zoey's hands shattered to the floor, water pooling around, a little of the glass's debris floating in the puddle. Michael could not look Zoey in her eyes and the shattered glass was the only excuse of not having to.

"I am so sorry, Mr. Osborne, I'll get you another glass of water—"

"That won't be necessary, Zoey." Michael interrupted her, stopping her in her tracks, finally able to get himself to utter words.

It was all beginning to make sense, now. Luca Giovanni's plans of *making him pay* were heavily afoot and he had been playing into his game all along. He was able to connect the dots with scribbly lines rather too quickly.

It was explosives. Luca had Michael deliver explosives to New Mercy…

BEDI

Parvati was on her way to Osborne investments to arrest Michael Osborne. She had no intention of calling him by that revered name. As far as she was concerned, he was Michael Morano to her.

Johnny stopped the car right outside. From the looks of the building, no one was there. It was empty, a gleaming tower of green glass windows and unlit rooms inside. The morning news had been the right kind of incentive of securing an arrest warrant for Michael Osborne. His superiors at the bureau were still having a hard time connecting philanthropic Michael Osborne to the disappeared Michael Morano. While Solonik might have died, Parvati was confident she could get Morano to spill the truth.

He had been smart in the beginning. But now… now he was hers.

OSBORNE

BLAM.

Michael had not been expecting the police. Let alone the bureau. But he guessed Luca had been thorough in his plans for him. There were two of them, a man and a woman. He had sent his employees back home but Zoey had insisted she stay with him. Whatever her intentions, he was glad of her offer.

"Mr. Osborne, I come bearing a warrant for your arrest." Said the woman. She was beautiful. Definitely Indian-American.

"There's been a mistake." Zoey said, trying to protest.

"Ma'am, please step aside." Said the male agent. "And let us do our jobs."

Zoey went quite right after. Michael didn't want to talk in front of Zoey. For his mind was still spinning with strategies of his own, trying to bring together how exactly Luca Giovanni had framed him for the bombing. The female agent came to stand behind him. She was taller than him. Whether it was the heels, Michael couldn't spare time to think.

For along with trying to figure out who had betrayed him and how exactly Luca Giovanni had screwed him, he was also mourning the deaths of all the 37 people that had died and the 18 injured critically at his hands.

BEDI

Michael Osborne had told her everything. Or so, he said he had.

"Either you think me a fool, Mr. *Osborne*, or your recent actions have deterred your ability to lie to an extent unknown to mankind." Parvati didn't believe Morano's fake account a bit. There were discrepancies he was clearing struggling to hide. So much for the FBI-level political assassin. What had gone wrong that was making him quaver so much. Not that he was quavering on the outside. Of course not. He was doing so on the inside and Parvati saw right through him.

Any other agent would have believed him word for word. But Parvati had Solonik's declaration on her side.

"You conveniently left the bit about changing your identity and moving to New York, leaving a dreadful past behind that has now caught up with you." Parvati said, not taking his non-sense for a second more. He fell silent at that.

"I bet you had silenced an... informant of mine who had tied you to your past identity upon my visit. Does the name Anna Solonik ring a bell?" Parvati asked him.

Again that face. Parvati heard some commotion on the outside. Surely it was Johnny giving those at this precinct a hard time. Parvati had chosen to bring Morano to a local station instead. It would help keep this case quiet since the station wasn't really a station but a front from the FBI for private interrogations like these.

Michael was his same, stone self.

"Maybe I was wrong to have asked my colleague sit this interrogation out. People are very... forthcoming when he does the honors." True, they did. But the only reason Parvati wanted him out was because she knew he wouldn't be able to handle Michael Morano. This man was a con-artist and a skilled one at that, fooling the entire country for two years. It stopped now.

"I have told you everything, Miss Bedi. Nothing more without my lawyer." Michael said. Lawyering up, are we? Parvati was satisfied at that. It meant she had Michael under her grasp. There was more of the commotion she had previously ignored. Parvati gave Michael a serious look and got up to go outside and inspect what has happening.

She turned around too late when Michael stood up, handcuffs undone, slamming tear gas on the ground where Parvati stood.

OSBORNE

"Never doubt me." Xavier said, immediately grabbing Michael into a hug.

"Alright, man, need to run," Michael said, trying to smile as best as he could at his old friend; the only from his old life that he had entrusted the truth with.

"You will get around Luca Givoanni's trap." Xavier said, driving Michael away.

Michael was a mess on the inside. He was fortunate, though, for the moment Luca's games had begun with that phone call, he had had Xavier track the entire situation. He had failed to warn him about the assassin, but had made up for it by helping him send the message he had to his family.

Before going to work in the morning, Michael had carried a tear gas bomb for a swift escape. It had come in hand. Agent Bedi was good. She had found Solonik. The only way she could have is if she herself was a client. Which had to be the case for no one was that good. Not even the FBI.

Michael had brought the rifle with which he had assassinated the senator upon Giovanni's order from Solonik, paying her handsomely for her silence. How could she have betrayed him? The woman rarely broke. But he was sure Agent Bedi and her partner must have broken her. But she had killed herself, like she always casually promised when her buyers asked for discretion. *I would kill myself before I tell any of those law enforces a word*.

Bedi must have been something for Solonik to reveal even a but of information. He felt sorry for her.

The poison had been Giovanni's choice. Now it made sense why. Michael had been sure to erase all traces of his being at Weston during the kill. But the poison, it seemed, left traces. That was how Parvati had gone to Solonik. How careless of him indeed.

The account and Ahmed Assef... surely they were connected to this somehow, too. Luca had trapped Michael in an elaborate cage, and he was only beginning to figure a way out. He had to have someone on the inside of Osborne. Michael was no fool...

"Hi, Michael," Corbin said from the other side as soon as Michael answered his call on the new burner Xavier had brought him.

"Tell me it wasn't her, Corbin. Tell me it wasn't her." Michael wanted so badly to be wrong.

"Well, it was. I have always wanted you to be wary of that… two-faced bitch." Corbin, now that he wasn't in a formal setting with Michael, was being himself, of course. "She alerted Agent Bedi to your activities last night. She got you arrested." Corbin said. Michael didn't know Zoey was capable of such treachery. But he had been a fool to not heed Corbin's advice about her.

"Yeah, well, I got him out." Xavier said from the driver's side.

"Oh, so that one's there, too." Corbin confirmed. Corbin had been friends with Michael ever since college. He was loyal just as much as Xavier was. But Zoey was not. She had been in league with Giovanni all this time…

"And listen to this. The account I was able to hack into, the one belonging to our Ahmed Assef? It's a front for Giovanni's illegal activity. He bought into your disaster recovery charity in order to frame you for the profitable aftermath of the bombing. The people in that hospital were insured by you, Michael. Share prices went up soon after the bombing. Luca made millions off framing you."

Son of a...

"Is it in the news yet?" Michael asked.

"No. Not yet. And thank the heavens miss Bedi had you secretly arrested. Your company and your reputation are safe. For now." Corbin said.

"We need to take care of those people first. Have another of my charities take care of their expenses and hospital bills." Michael had himself under control. He didn't want to break down in front of his friends. He would forever carry the guilt of the deaths he had caused. But for now, he needed a clear head to do what he was about to.

"Alright," Corbin said, without commenting. "What about our friend Zoey, your assistant? Can't have her ruining all our careers with that mouth of hers," Corbin finished.

"I'll take care of her. What will you do now, Michael?" Xavier asked.

Michael knew Agent Bedi was his best shot at finding Patricia and his daughter. After carefully concocting a plan, which took him about a minute, he was sure of both what he said and what he had planned.

"Get Miss Bedi to meet with me."

Chapter Eight

BEDI

Parvati was infuriated.

The news of Morano escaping would spread faster than fire itself. Parvati was sure of it. Even though it was more of Whitehill's fault for having been fooled outside by two "unidentified men," Parvati knew he would pour all the dirt over her. Since she was the rookie who got promoted at a station too high, it would be all the more easy for Whitehill to throw her under the bus to save his own skin and career.

She had gravely underestimated Morano. However had he cut loose the handcuffs she had so expertly tied his hands with? They taught you face expressions in the bureau and there had been not even a ghost of any across Morano's face.

He was good. He was damn good. It was this realization that made Parvati all the more angry.

Johnny came inside the interrogation room which Parvati had gone back into after the dust had settled. "Anything from facial recognition? The cameras caught their faces, did they not?" Parvati asked him.

"One of the two was a hacker. Or maybe they had a third outside who hacked into the security detail of this precinct. All footage from the last three hours is gone." Johnny said, disappointment all across his face. Parvati didn't notice how to-the-point he had gotten. He wasn't giving her a hard time or pissing her off. It *was* his fault and he had, out of the blue, found the decency to shut up, for once.

"What do we do now?" Whitehill asked.

"We go home. We sleep. We come back tomorrow to catch that bastard."

Parvati returned home and took a shower. The hot of the water always helped her unclench her stressed up muscles knotted up. The memory of her first hot bath always came to her whenever she bathed; she had been scared then, but had learned to overcome the heat. Years later, it was perhaps her only source of calm and peace of mind.

She came out into her bedroom, her clothes lined on the bed. She needed a drink.

Walking her way to the freezer in the living room, a chill caught her. The heat was up and she had only recently taken a burning hot shower. Taking a look at the windows, she learned they were shut.

It was not air that had crept up her spine. It was... anxiety.

The superiors at the bureau were not stupid. They would be able to tell after one of their infamous sweeps who had let their suspect go. While Whitehill would have the favor of most on the board, Parvati knew logic would help her win. She never made these mistakes. Had she been the one outside the interrogation door, she would not have let them fool her like Whitehill had been fooled. Morano would still be in their custody and she would, instead of pouring herself a glass of diet coke like she was now, be interrogating Morano with the very ice she now felt ebbing and flowing her every fiber as she drank.

CLICK CLICK.

Parvati turned around. The lights in her living room had flickered on and off all of a sudden. Her house was completely submerged in dark, the light from the moonlit sky outside and the lampposts lighting up enough of her way to move around. She preferred it that way. It saved her up from extra utility, too. It probably was something in the wiring, she assured herself.

But it happened again.

Parvati walked to the lights near her TV which had flickered. She stared, squinting, into the bulbs. Nothing seemed to be wrong with them. She checked the switchboard; the switches were off, too.

Weird.

Seconds later, her phone lit up. She hadn't even realized she had left it on the TV table when on her way to her room for her shower. There was a text from an unknown number.

WE NEED 2 TALK.

RECEIVED: 11:13 PM

What the hell? The same chill from before crept up her spine. The bath towel firmed wrapped around her was meagre protection from this... weird cold. She quickly wrote back.

WHO IS THIS? SENT: 11:15 PM

The *ting* of her outgoing message brought her more anxiety than sense of control. She waited for a response, but her mystery text-messager, it seemed, had suddenly run out of words. It was very unlikely for this person to be a prankster for all of those were filtered out on her phone. Someone had gone to great lengths to obtain her phone number.

Or, none at all, Parvati thought, as a reply finally came.

MICHAEL MORANO. I NEED YOUR HELP...

RECEIVED:

11:20 PM

MORANO

THEN

Michael woke up.

The ceiling fan was the first thing he saw. He tilted his head to his right and was reminded of how amazing last night had been. Patricia lay in the covers, her black curls splayed across her pillow. She looked beautiful even in sleep.

Michael exhaled, preparing to get up. It was then that he noticed his hand was interlocked with one of Patricia's.

They had slept with their hands intertwined.

Michael didn't want to break that connection, so he decided against getting up and going out. Instead, he lay as he had been.

Patricia…

Good things didn't come to Michael Morano very often. The dark mists and clouds that surrounded his family rarely left him and kept anything at bay. It was a vicious cycle, of hatred, enmity, crime, and war. But Patricia was the best. She was the one thing that had seen him not for where he came from or what he represented, but who he was and what was inside of him.

No one had ever tried to look past him like this.

Michael had found her soulmate.

MONELLO

THEN

Patrick Monello was worried sick.

His dealer had bailed on him again and he had spent three days without a supply of drugs. His withdrawal had already begun kicking in. Since it was the beginning, it was easy to hide the symptoms from his mother. But Patrick had both seen and researched how users trying to get better, undergoing withdrawal got like physically and mentally.

He blamed his father for everything.

His mother had been on to him ever since she had found out about the affair. A year had gone by. Then two. Both Patrick and his mother had one day found the courage to confront him about all the "late nights at work" and the "busier-than-usual" weekends.

Patrick's father had filed for divorce the very next day.

While his mother was working two jobs to make ends meet and they were getting by, education in the US, much to their bad luck and discomfort, was too expensive. His mother wanted him well-educated, and later successful and financially able and didn't want to just keep on paying their bills and maintaining a roof over their heads. Which was why she had taken loans and what not so that Patrick could continue his studies.

But Patrick was no fool.

His mother was struggling now and Patrick's job at the smoothie store in their area was not putting the dent needed.

Drugs had come as a relief from all the stress and depression.

When some kids at school who were try to "corrupt the dorks" had found Patrick, he had been too easy a target. And so, Patrick's relationship with drugs had begun.

But the kids who appeared to him today at school were much older.

"You are Patrick Monello, are you not?" Of the three that had approached him, the muscular one in the middle has spoken up.

"Yes, who are you?" Patrick asked him.

"Friend of Rocky's," the muscular one had said. Patrick allowed himself to relax. Rocky was his dealer and must have sent a replacement. That explained his being late.

"You got the cash?" the muscular guy asked him.

"Yeah..." Patrick nervously looked around for anyone looking at them suspiciously. Richmond High was infamous for drugs and

an even popular site for local drug dealers, specifically mafia kids too young to participate in their family's "businesses," for selling. Everyone involved had to be careful.

"Here," Patrick said, handing the muscular one a thick wad of cash. His business associates took a look of the thick wad and scoffed at him, sizing him up from bottom to top.

"Woah, kid. No way you're this loaded. Where'd you steal this money from?" the muscular guy asked him. These kids stayed away from people whose appearances and money didn't add up. Patrick was not new to this and was expecting it.

"There is more where that came from. Just give me the damn product," Patrick said, already impatient from the withdrawal.

They all looked at each other, and after a few seconds of uncertainty, the muscular guy took out a garbage back from his bag which had the contents Patrick was buying. He took *it from him as if it was the last supply of food on the planet, shoving it in his own bag.*

Sadly, for Mrs. Monello, Patrick's education was not the only reason she was struggling and taking in loans...

"You know Michael Morano?" the muscular guy asked him out of nowhere.

"Um, yeah, he's a friend. What of him?" Patrick knew something was wrong. Michael, wasn't just his friend but his best friend. He was from the Morano family pretty famous for fights and a well-flourishing business.

"Nothing, nothing at all," he said.

Patrick also dismissed it. He had to get back home before his mother and enjoy his purchase. He shook hands with the guy. As an afterthought, he asked him, "What was your name? Didn't catch it."

"Tommy Giovanni," said the muscular guy. "Enjoy your purchase, kid, it will send you straight to heaven."

The trio walked away, laughing in the distance.

MORANO

Michael was driving to the abandoned factory Giovanni had messaged him to "meet" at.

The moment Giovanni had called him to inform his little friend had been taken care of, *Michael had lost it. He had gone to Patrick's house. Patrick's mother said he wasn't home, but Michael had got in with an excuse to "look for a science book he had lent Patrick." Mrs. Monello had let him up, unaware that Patrick was in his room, lying OD-ed on the floor.*

Patrick had cried too loud, not being able to keep it in. Mrs. Monello had seen him, and later Patrick. She had began sobbing, too, first into Michael's arms, then by the nearest wall. After what had felt like a very long time, she had stopped. Michael had become weary, who knew what an ailing mother who had seen her son lying dead on the floor could do all of a sudden? He was suddenly ready to prevent her from hurting herself.

Instead, she said something.

"Michael Morano... you had my baby killed."

"No, Mrs. Morano, it wasn't—"

"It. WAS. YOU!"

The shouting that followed was too painful for Michael to hear. He had left immediately. When next he was getting into his car, he had taken out his phone and called all of the Blood Lords, sparing them the details of the sudden call to arms, but saying just the right thing to get them riled up for the fight.

Michael was going to beat Giovanni to a bloody pulp.

The factory was a fifteen-minute drive away, yet he drove as fast he could, the rush of battle too intoxicating to ignore. The other

Blood Lords, Loution, Joey, Eddie, Paul, Rob, Matt, John, and Richie were on their way, he could tell from his rear view, in two land rovers.

Michael could see the factory in the distance and four vehicles. Tommy Giovanni stood by his electric green, expensive sedan, arms folded. He could tell, even from the distance that was between them, that the bastard was smirking at him.

He wouldn't be as soon as he was done with him.

"I see you've brought quite the party with you, Morano. I thought we were just going to chat," Tommy said.

"So, have you," said Loution.

"I will speak only to the man in charge, sorry, Lou," Tommy taunted Loution. Technically, Loution Morano was the Blood Lord's leader since he was the oldest. But it was Michael whom everybody listened to. Loution, however, was much more mature than all

the guys standing on both the sides combined. He said nothing.

"You know why we're here, Giovanni," Michael said in hauntingly low tone.

"Of course, I do, your little buddy like his present alright?"

It was not wise of Michael to have started the fight... but Tommy had left him no choice. The drugs, killing Patrick... the grounds for "not being the first to raise the gun" as per their late grandfather's instructions were too past soiled now to be followed.

Michael had run into Tommy, pushing then shoving him to the ground from the impact of his hard-paced running. They both had fallen on the ground, which had started the whole fiasco. Michael could see from the corner of his eye that guys on both the sides had already begun fighting as he sent a punch into Tommy's face.

"I will dismember you, Morano," Tommy said.

"And I will kill you, Giovanni," Michael said.

Tommy shoved Michael off him and quickly got up, send a kicking into Michael's chest. He groaned getting up, but was quick, too. No room for giving the bastard any edge on him. Punch, swing, kick. Punch, kick, swing. On and on went their dance.

"Tired, Morano? Already?" Tommy taunted Michael, panting and backing away.

Michael kept walking toward him. It was pissing him off why the bastard was backing away. He was too angry to even see it: Tommy was scared. They had been in fights before. Michael had never lost. Michael did not know it, of course, but Tommy had seen something in his eyes. The look of someone willing to kill.

It was their most sacred rule for generations, keeping the Moranos and the Giovannis, sworn enemies of each other, at peace and away from each other's businesses. No mafia man under the age of 30 was to kill another. No matter how bad the fight got. It ran their businesses without bloodshed. When the men passed thirty, they reached the maturity the elders had when they came up with the rule and would never go that far. Ever.

"Come here and face me like a man, you—"

CLICK.

Before Michael has been able to utter the obscenity he had in mind for Tommy, the coward had taken out a gun from the waist band of his jeans. Michael was shocked more at his having failed at spotting the gun jutting out of Tommy's bomber jacket during their fight than he was at the gun itself.

No one brought a gun to a fight, another rule.

"What's the matter, huh? You scared? You scared I'm going to kill you?" Tommy said. He did well to hide his stutter. But Michael saw right through him. The bastard knew what he was getting into and had brought a gun to level the playing field.

Everyone, both Morano and Giovanni, had stopped fighting. They were all staring at the gun, not even Tommy. Michael didn't care one bit about the gun and started walking a surprisingly casual walk towards Tommy. There were murmurs from the others at Michael's show of bravado.

"Back off, Morano, or I will shoot you!" Tommy kept on taking a step behind, albeit slowly; he was scared. "I said back OFF!" But Michael wasn't listening. His cousins, the other Blood Lords, were shouting at him to walk away.

All Michael did was leapt the remaining distance at Tommy, falling on top of him. They struggled for the gun aggressively. Neither man gave up—Michael, because of the anger of having lost his little brother; Tommy because of fear. But the thing with struggles is, they do not go on for very long. Eventually, some conceits. Eventually, someone loses.

Eventually, someone wins.

BANG, went the bullet.

OSBORNE

NOW

Michael and Corbin were impressed by their handiwork. Or maybe it was dumb luck how the FBI agent had chosen to hear them out and not shoot them there and then. She was pretty, Michael thought. But beauty could be deceiving, something Michael could tell this detective used to her advantage.

They had unwillingly entered her home. She had refused to enter their car, which was fair, Michael thought. She had taken a while to respond. From the still-wet hair that clung to her neck, slick with water, and back, he could tell she must have been showering and that this interference was "inopportune."

But Michael had no choice.

"Well," she said, breaking the ice, "talk."

115

Michael heaved a sigh and began from the start. That his family was as dark as families like his came. That, even when they were little, they were raised with only a single purpose: to bring pride and honor to their family.

"How exactly?" the detective interrupted him.

"By securing or acquiring more power through whatever means necessary," Michael told her at which she fell silent. Michael saw hope in those eyes; he needed her to believe him. So, he continued with Tommy Giovanni and his "supplying" Patrick with drugs that had led to his OD-ing. He skipped out on how Mrs. Monello had cried on his shoulder. He could tell she had sensed he was skipping on details. But she didn't stop him.

He next told her about the fight and how he and Tommy had struggled for the gun. He told her that it had been an accident and that no one had really aimed at the other. The gun's trigger got pressed by a collective effort on Tommy and his part and that he had been the fortunate one not facing the bullet-end.

"Am I to believe it an accident?" She asked him.

"All of the Blood Lords who could corroborated my claim have been murdered," Michael told her. "I am sure you can get the truth from Tommy's guys once you track them down," he added.

"I plan to, Morano, but don't stop on my account. What happened then?" She was looking at all the documentation and proof, or whatever of it he had been able to provide her with, of his innocence.

He continued.

"I ran away... disappeared. Changed my name and identity. I changed myself," he said. He told her about old man Osborne and how he had taken him in and how, with the money he had left him both when alive and in his will when he had died, he had started his finance firm from the ground up.

"How you managed it without any involvement from your mafia family or contacts is beyond me, Morano, but that is not important," the detective said.

Michael told her about Richie and how he had come with death reports of all the other Blood Lords. He told her he had dismissed his cries for help and had, the very next day, regretted having done so in the first place.

"He got to him, too," Michael told detective Bedi.

The detective was taking it all in, starting to see how exactly Luca Giovanni was trying to get back at the Blood Lords for the murder of his son.

"So, your cousins died because of a crime you committed," she said matter-of-factly.

"It was an accident," Michael reminded her.

The detective tucked away a lose curl of hair behind her ear, sighing her impatience. Corbin was getting uncomfortable and Michael could sense it coming off him. He had said nothing through the discussion so far and it wasn't like him to stay quiet. For this long.

She gave them both a look which was Michael's cue to carry on.

He told her, next, about the call. How Giovanni had figured out who he was now and where. He had kidnapped his ex-girlfriend and had her talk to him on the phone. He told her that he had no choice but to go ahead with his plans and whatever he told him the moment he learned that he had a daughter with Patricia.

"Hanna. She had named her Hanna… after my grandmother. And I had left her," Michael said. He didn't care what the detective thought of him at this display of intimacy; he wanted the truth out. He had held on to it all these years. Even after he

119

had found out about his daughter, he had not let his true emotions flow.

But he couldn't help himself now.

Detective Bedi was looking at his face with renewed interest. Michael didn't cry, not even when he was little. In fact, he was a quiet kid if the accounts from his aunts he heard about him were credible at all.

Michael held himself with great restraint, yet a single tear escaped him, trickling down his cheek having given him away.

"Michael, what did he say?" she asked him, kind enough to not kick him while he was already on the ground.

"He said he would kill them if I didn't do as he said."

BEDI

Parvati heard him without interrupting. Everything he was saying was adding up, and it wasn't much comfort for this one had the audacity to first escape from right under her nose then text her to "meet up" because he needed "help."

"Corbin" sat next to him. He seemed like the nerdy initiates at the FBI that Parvati had worked with. One look at him and she knew of the two, he was not capable of fighting. You had only one talent; either brains or brawn. But Michael Morano, had both, it seemed.

"It was Giovanni who had me buy my rifle from Solonik," he had answered. "The powder was probably one way for him to get me caught," he told her.

The poison used left some residue after a few hours of having been shot through a firearm. Luca Giovanni, he had also revealed, was one of her very loyal customers. She would do anything to protect his identity so that her other "business partners" would continue her work without his involvement compromised. So, he had not killed her. It added up.

Morano had next told him of the money Luca had him transfer into an unknown and how, Corbin had found out, the very next the same amount being used to buy shares of the Osborne's disaster relief firm. When he had gone to check whether this Assef guy was legit, his wife had answered which he now believed was a set up. His assistant, Zoey, had done the mix up making it look like Michael had put in money into his own firm to profit off the bombing at the children's hospital which his firm covered. Corbin had shown her the access feeds and the poorly attempted hack at the name.

Parvati had been right about the bridge. Michael Morano was connected to it. He told her that his family had sent an assassin to avenge the deaths of their sons, his cousins, and that he had led him away from NYU. He had some nerve mentioning the "gift" he had sent back to Enzo Morano. If Parvati was

122

good at what she did, she knew he was trying to earn her trust outing himself like this. All the evidence added up, too…

The bomb however, was too much.

He told her he had had no idea that it had been explosives Luca was having him deliver. Nothing to worry about, though. She would get to the bottom of any lie he had told.

For an ex-con, though, he had not lied and was pretty convincing.

He finally finished, and Parvati let there be a modicum of silence. It was moments like these, after the guilty party had said their piece and were waiting to either be dismissed or believed, that you could tell whether they were lying. It showed in their face. The anticipation.

She had to give it to Luca Giovanni. The trap he had lain was quite elaborate. Having Morano do chores and what not all in the guise of just being able to do whatever he could with him for he owned him. Yet every errand had been related to the master plan. Luca had had Morano seal his own fate.

The assassination, the account and the money later the bombing to make off millions off his own disaster relief firm with a disaster also of his own...

She had everything she needed to bring Morano down. The record for the assassination, the money put into his firm and the bombing. She was debating whether Michael had been smart at all reaching out to her like he had. Not to mention hacking into her electricity system and their little stunt with the lights. Meddling with a federal agent like they had was a criminal offence.

Not only had he confessed to everything, whether it was a clarification of his innocence or him admitting to his outright did not matter, he had also given her more to bring him down for good.

This case would give her that boost that she now realized she had needed. The promotion would not only mean an advanced career, but her being bumped up to management. That would mean no more Johnny not-so-English and his constant, idiotic put-downs.

But she looked into Morano's face and saw nothing short of innocence. She saw in him a scared teenager who had run away from the darkness of his family and tried to make a life of his own. Had it been any other family, he would have been able to escape them permanently. But the Mafia didn't let anyone escape, be it their enemy or blood.

"Will you help me rescue my family?" He asked her.

Parvati had apprehended countless fugitives and criminals by now and this case had turned out to be different. She had it in the bag. And she also didn't. Were she to officially take all the records Morano and his sidekick had provided and everything he had confessed, she would have reason, motive, and legal obligation to open an investigation into Luca Giovanni.

She wasn't done yet.

Parvati had sworn to protect the innocent from the evils of this world. People in her line of work often forgot that for the money and the promotions were the only thing they cared about. But Parvati wasn't like that. She was different. And here was a man asking for help to save his family.

What came out next of Parvati's mouth, she knew, was of steadiness and firm resolve.

"I will."

Chapter Nine

BEDI

"Your plan is a failure of epic proportions," Parvati said.

The detective had "allowed" them to stay over at her place. Michael had refrained from providing his opinion on the decision neither had Corbin asked for any permission. Parvati Bedi—it turned out she had a first name, too—was bossy like that, Michael had gathered. Or maybe it was an impression he had misinterpreted? That had to be it.

Parvati Bedi was too… sweet-looking and reserved, too professional to send any vibe unintentionally. He knew how they were trained at the bureau; one of the many things you learned to understand if you knew how to use your mafia family resources to your advantage. Besides, with agency resources, they would be able to get to Luca Giovanni much faster.

Not that Corbin needed any help from the FBI.

"What exactly are you trying to say, detective?" Corbin asked. That was about as much respectable as he was going to get. He didn't like people questioning him or his work in any way.

"I am saying, you will get us all killed," she said, tucking a stray lock of hair behind her ear, "you cannot expect me to allow you to walk into what is probably a fortress." She looked at Michael for support. He didn't want to look directly in her eyes thanks to his micro-meltdown. He would have to confront the woman at some point, and that point was fast approaching—it was probably already here—since it would take only an act of God to get Corbin and her to play along.

"She is right, Corbin," Michael finally intervened. "You did great, locating Luca—"

"—I didn't do *just* great," Corbin interrupted, "I did… I did *great* great." Michael kept himself from snorting at Corbin's temporary aridity of vocabulary words needed to praise himself. While he knew it was only temporary, it had been a little treat watching him struggle. And even more a treat watching Parvati stare at him.

"Your locating Luca Giovanni was indeed amazing, Mr. Corbin, we could use someone like you at the bureau," Parvati said. Meanwhile, Michael got a glimpse of Corbin's mind: *hell yes, bitch. Your bureau failed you, but I found that SOB within 47 seconds*.

"Thanks, but no thanks," came Corbin's reply.

"But as it stands," Parvati continued from where she had left off, nothing short of irritation on her face as if trying to reprimand an errant toddler, "going blind into that abandoned warehouse is suicide. Since we are not getting anyone from the bureau involved physically, it is just us three, and, um, your other *associate*." Parvati was, of course, talking about Xavier, who had gone to "deal" with Zoey, his traitorous PA.

They were running out of time.

"That seems like a perfect team," Michael said. "Small, quiet, we will go in, extract, kill, get out." Michael was a master tactician and saying what he just had made feel like some super heroes stuck up boss. Of course, it sounded ridiculous.

"What about being ambushed by his security—"

"—You will want to carry this plan out with us, detective," Michael said, cutting Parvati off in the middle, something he had observed she didn't mind, "when you learn of Corbin's other capabilities."

OSBORNE

"How did you…" Parvati trailed off.

They had been able to convince the detective to let them go ahead with their plan. She had been amazed, of course, upon hearing Corbin could track heat signatures via satellite, one that Michael had had secretly launched up. There is a lot he had done ever since he had left his cursed family.

"When did you…" the poor detective, it seemed, was at a loss of words.

They had packed up pretty good for what was to come. It was now or never. Michael was done with Giovanni and this ended today. So, they waited for their next move outside of the abandoned warehouse in Parvati's car.

It was the very warehouse where it had gone down between him and Tommy…

"Is it even legal—"

"—Okay! So, I can see four men on the first floor, eight on the second…" Corbin went on with his heat signatures and what exactly they would need to do to clear out all possible threats. Parvati only patiently listened. But her silence didn't surprise him anymore. Neither did her not reacting to being cut off mid-sentence.

As for the satellite being legal, well…

"That's almost a tactical unit in there! We are but three people," Parvati said. She looked at Corbin with a raised eyebrow, something he knew he would enjoy as it undid Corbin's own facial expressions. "Do you even know how to shoot?"

"No," Corbin said, matter-of-factly. "I will stay behind and help from here."

"I had figured," Parvati said.

These two were really hitting it off.

Michael couldn't believe he was finally going to rescue Patricia and his daughter.

Hanna…

Did Giovanni know they were on to him? Corbin had never failed him. They had an FBI agent in their car for crying out loud. This shouldn't be too much of anything. But then again, the assassin had been all but one person. Michael remembered what it was like when it was two mafia armies against each other. In their case, it was just two against twenty.

Well, two and a half.

A car came from around a corner. This was unexpected. It was a blue sedan. Xavier's sedan.

"What is he doing here? I thought we were incognito?" Corbin complained.

"Incognito?" Parvati scoffed. "With that loudspeaker mouth of yours?"

"Hush, you two!" Michael silenced them both as Xavier stopped against Parvati's car. He rolled down his window and Michael spoke to him from the passenger seat.

"Your assistant won't be bothering you again," Xavier said.

"What is that supposed to mean?" Parvati quirked at his revelation.

"It means," Xavier said, sliding his shades down to look at Michael, "that she is alive. But is secretly wishing she isn't." Xavier wouldn't go that far, of course. Neither would he. Wherever Zoey was, she was okay; Michael guessed Xavier must have given her a scare of a lifetime or something. *I'll fire her ass*, Michael made himself a mental note.

"Guys! Guys!" Corbin bought their attention. "Four of Giovanni's men are heading this way. They are on the second floor."

"What?!" Parvati said. "I thought you were monitoring them!"

"I was," Corbin said. "Then big bull here," he motioned at Xavier with both hands to put emphasis on his words, "showed up and then I wasn't."

"Why am I stuck with these clowns, God I must have done something wrong," Parvati mumbled to herself but was audible enough for them to hear. Xavier laughed a huff. "Morano, check your phone; is your GPS on?" She asked Michael.

He checked his phone. It was on.

"That's impossible!" Michael protested. This was the most basic rule of them all. He never left his GPS on when *out* like this. Also, never.

"It seems their nerd out-smarted our nerd," Parvati said, "of course, they have a hacker on their side!"

Shit. Luca was on to them now.

"If you clowns value your lives, listen to me very carefully," Parvati began.

"I like this one," Xavier said. Parvati ignored him.

"Corbin, take Michael's phone and drive away with… big bull here," she had paused momentarily, she didn't know Xavier's name. Big bull kind of suited him. "Make sure those men follow your car." She instructed. "Stay in touch with Morano and me via comms."

Detective Bedi was saving them from their deaths.

"Morano, come with me," she told Michael, getting out of the car and heading for the trunk to retrieve their duffel bag that they had stashed with ammo and guns. "Let's take that son of a bitch *down*."

Or was she doing death's work for him?

BEDI

Parvati had her gun ready by her thigh. Morano was tailing her with one of his own.

She couldn't believe she had let herself be talked into what was the worst EXFIL plan she had come across in all her time at work. The idiots wanted her to just *walk in* the stupid warehouse. And she was doing exactly that.

She let herself admit, she missed Johnny.

With a gesture of her hand, she told Michael to *check the room on the other side while she checked the one on the right*. She knew he understood her when he nodded and went looking. Better Morano than that narcissistic nerd, Parvati thought.

So, she began looking.

Their strategy was to clear and ascend, a classic they were taught in their very first year of the academy. This was *Luca Giovanni's* hideout they were crashing. She wouldn't normally barge into a death trap like this. They had had no choice. Thanks to Morano's idiot aides.

Nothing but old, rusty, broken machinery, the place was an abandoned dump. She wondered why construction companies had left a structure as old as this standing this long. Then, she didn't need to. It was

Giovanni's personal little haven. The first thing she was going to do when she arrested him and they rescued that little girl and her mom, Parvati thought, would be to tear this damn factory to pieces.

SMACK.

It was the sound of a bottle hitting and shattering on the floor.

Parvati had company.

As graceful as a cat would be in a situation like this, she ducked for cover, slamming her back into a wall. She could peak outside into the main hall of the floor she was on. Heavy footsteps accompanied an even heavier voice.

"Come on out and play, little kitty. We saw you climb the stairs up to here."

She knew which one of them she was taking down first. She had to be smart with her bullets, though. She had left the duffel in Morano's hands and yet had enough rounds to last her this fight. It was second nature for her to organize even her ammunition and use it sparingly.

"What's the matter, beautiful, can't take us buffs with all your fancy-ass training?" Laughter followed. It was the same man who had spoken before. So, they knew she was from the bureau. They weren't supposed to…

So many things had gone wrong. And so many were yet to. Parvati reigned her anger in.

"I bet your ass isn't the only fancy thing about ya', 'eh?" More, roaring laughter. *Grrr…*

 Parvati silently stepped out from her cover, hands in the air, walking toward them.

"We have ourselves a nice one 'ere," said a different man this time. It was all the distraction she needed to, swiftly like lightning, retrieve her gun from her jeans and unleash a round of bullets on the bastards.

"Oye!" One of them shouted.

She got two of them, hitting one in the head and the other through his chest. No sign of the third man. Had she miscalculated before?

Get your act together, Bedi.

"You die. Today."

While Parvati was confident it was him was going to die by her hand, she was amazed at how fast time had flown and that the sun was past up.

The oversized *girl* began with a punch. Parvati had minor trouble dodging him. His arms were longer, as was his height. He swung again and Parvati dodged. She took advantage of his having lost momentum and hit him in the back of his knee.

Hard.

"Aaaaah!" He knelt down upon the same knew by reflex, the pain of it thudding into the ground shot soon after and that gave

140

Parvati the time she needed to swerve and spin-kick into his face.

Also, hard.

The man hit the floor, thudding once and never getting up. Why use one's gun when you could knock them out cold?

Parvati ran for the other side where Morano had gone. It was too quiet there and she sensed foul play.

OSBORNE

They had caught Michael not two seconds later.

He had not been able to move, since it was two of their most muscular by the feel of their arms, who taken one of Michael's arms each. A third one had shown up, and had kicked him in the chest, then stomach. Those were military boots the bastard had on and they knocked the breath out of him.

Michael had groaned. But no hard enough, it seemed, for Military Boots had hit him again, albeit once.

He was being dragged upstairs. His knees kept banging on the stairwell but he didn't let them get any satisfaction off him.

They reached, soon, what was the top most floor for there was nothing but a dirty ceiling with tearing paint Michael could see before they took him inside. He looked around for numbers, out of habit. There were more than twenty men in there. Corbin never failed him. He trusted him. These men had got in here some other way, Michael wagered.

The center of attention of everyone present, though, and soon Michael's, too, was the man seated on a black sofa, all black-clad. He held a cigar in his mouth and stared at him playfully.

Michael was dropped rather harshly on the ground by the man's feet. He tried to get up but kicked in the back. Groaning, he looked up to the man, who with the motion of his hand, asked his men to back off. With the same hand, he motioned for Michael to look to his left.

There were two bodies on the floor where he had made him look. A woman and a girl, hands and mouths tied. They were unconscious.

It was Patricia and his daughter, Hanna.

"Don't worry," Luca Giovanni said, taking away his cigar from his mouth, "they are still alive." A little of Michael's panicking died upon hearing that.

"Now tell me, boy," he said, "how shall we do this?"

Chapter Ten

MORANO

THEN

Michael ran from the scene.

It had been an accident. Of course, it was an accident. Michael only wanted the gun. He was going to throw it far away from Tommy's reach so he could watch him back up, scared as he was of Michael.

Tommy Giovanni. He had been tenacious with the gun. It was his gun and he knew it better. Of course, he was easily able to slide the gun from Michael's grip.

That was when Michael had punched him and taken it away. It was when he was forcing it out his hand that the he had pulled the trigger.

Blood. There had been blood everywhere. Giovanni was practically soaked in it. His hair, face...

Blood. *There was blood on Michael's clothes, too.*

There was no one around these parts. It was either his luck or fate was playing a cruel game with him. He had to get rid of these bloody clothes. He took off his button-down. The t-shirt he wore underneath, luckily, was blood-free. There was still blood on his jeans. He untucked his t-shirt out and covered the blood-soaked area on his jeans with it. He wiped his arms and face with his button-down and threw in a dumpster that was there.

He saw a homeless man throw the shirt.

Had he seen the blood on it? Shit...

Michael relaxed himself. And walked away. Turning around, he realized the homeless man had just been waiting for him to leave so he could take the shirt out of the dumpster and take it.

He had no idea where he was. But he sure was back among the living for there had been no one around those parts. It was an abandoned factory, of course. Not even users and addicts went there.

He had got lucky.

There was a park nearby that his eyes had spotted. Michael decided to go to it. He needed to sit down. All the crazy running had tired him. He found an abandoned seat close to where a bunch of children were giddily riding the swings.

He sat down.

Sighing a sigh of relief, he tried to wrap his head around what exactly had happened.

He had killed Tommy Giovanni, heir to the Giovanni family and son of Luca Giovanni, their family's sworn enemies. They wouldn't care whether it was an accident. Luca would have his head, and many others, for what he had done to his son.

He had to disappear.

Michael had always wanted to run away from his family. But like this?

He had no other option. It was either run away and live, or go back and die.

But could he really escape Luca Giovanni?

He was damn well going to try.

"I have nowhere to go."

Michael had run to the first person he could think of. Old man Osborne. He ran a whole operation of rescuing runaways from mafia families and was often seen at their high school, and any other events schools like his (where kids from mafia families came to study) donating and doing charity, while secretly pitching his plan to those who had already reached out to him.

He had his sources.

Michael had never reached out to him before, of course. He was the Morano heir, son of Frederick Morano. Next in line to inherit the empire, his father and uncles had always kept a close eye on him; one to ensure the seat of power was transferred to him when the time came, the others to ensure they stole from him the heritage that was to be his.

They could have it for all he cared. He had wanted out.

Maybe this was his only chance.

"Boy, tell me," old man Osborne asked, "have you left your past behind? Or has some of it made its way here with you?"

Michael didn't really know why they called him old man Osborne. He was an octogenarian, yes. But there was more to that than everybody let on. As for his past having followed him here, he knew exactly what Osborne was asking of him: have you run away even or at a cost.

He had murdered his enemy's son...

"I am all alone," Michael lied.

OSBORNE

NOW

"You thought you ran away from your sin?" Luca said. "You were wrong, boy. Dead wrong."

Michael had quickly scanned the room again. There were about twenty of Giovanni's men, standing around him in a wide circle as if he was some circus animal, ready to perform. There was no way he could take them all at once.

"You thought you were getting ahead every step of the way, when I was ten steps further all the time," Luca said.

Michael looked up at him. He had aged well. White hair and beard, he sat on that sofa as if he owned the world in his suit. He looked around, there was no sign of Patricia and Hanna... They had *just* been there!

"Please," Michael said, "let them go. It is me you want."

"The Giovanni have morals, Morano," Luca said. "When men fight, they fight with men and among men." He stood up from his seat, and walked his way to Michael.

WHACK.

His foot met with his face and Michael spat blood on the ground.

"I want you to feel pain. Before I make you watch them bleed."

Sick bastard.

"Stand up, and defend your worthless ass," Luca said. And, as if on cue, his goons began circulating him. He had fought before. But it had been a long time. And these twenty, by the looks of them, seemed to be Giovanni's finest. They would kill him with their mere hands.

But Michael had been chosen as the Morano heir for a reason. And being Frederick Morano's son had nothing to do with it. All the men, when deemed of a worthy age, in the Morano family were to fight each other. It didn't matter who fought whom, and whether they formed teams. Whoever stood standing by the end of the fight was the heir.

All of his cousins had turned on him. He had fended them all of. If he could fight off seven men and survive, fighting twenty was not impossible.

He had something far more important to lose today unlike in the fight he had with his cousins.

His family.

The first guy came running at him and swung a punch at him. Michael dodged at the right time, ducking out of the way then grabbing him from behind and twisting his neck and head in one complete motion.

He fell, neck broken, down to the ground. Dead.

It was two at a time after that. Punch and kick. Punch and kick. Dodge.

It wasn't a fair fight. They had taken out weapons. Metal knuckles, chains, blades. Michael had received his share of bruises and cuts. It was when one man had slashed across his cheek with his blade that Michael had found the opportunity to snatch that blade from him.

In one small motion, he had slit the man's throat, leaving him to bleed to death.

Two came from behind him and tried to take his arms in control. When one took control of his left arm, he pushed against it, lifting himself off the ground, arching his way to the man's back, and closing in on his neck with his legs and locking them in. He twisted his thighs to deliver him death; they both fell, only one lifeless.

His counterpart came in with a back hand which Michael dodged.

ZZZAAPP!

"Aahhh!" Michael backed away. He had been hit with a high-voltage electric taser from the looks of it. It hurt a great deal, where he had been struck with the taser. It had to be military-grade.

Michael was on the defensive now. It was a series of ducks and dodges. Whatever, happened, he had to avoid being hit by that monstrosity. He knew he would buckle if he came into contact with it again.

"You will not walk out of here alive, Morano," Luca said. From where, Michael had no idea. But he could hear him. One hit from the taser baton and he would not be able to fight. "You made a mistake going after the king, young prince."

It was the thought of his daughter that lent him the strength to run into the man that held the taser baton. And it was luck—pure luck—how the fully powered current missed him as he tackled the man down, forcing the baton out of his hand, and slamming it into his neck.

He screamed an ear-splitting scream before going numb. Dead.

WHACK.

Someone hit Michael at the back of his head and he fell on top of his recent kill. Michael had not gone under and could feel his body being dragged away by two powerful arms. They were taking him to Luca, who now stood starting him dead in the face. He had taken off his jacket, and rolled up his sleeves.

"Kneel before me." He said in a dangerously low voice.

His knees gave way under him as the men who had carried him hit him behind each. Michael fell to his knees, head bowed.

Thirteen. He had killed thirteen men.

SLAM.

Michael spat blood on the floor as Luca kicked him in the guts.

He didn't know it whether it was that kick that reminded him he had not come alone, or something else. Where was detective Parvati? Funny how the one fed he had come across was not here when he needed her the most.

Maybe she was working an angle? She was a *federal agent* for crying out loud. She was definitely working an angle.

But death stood in front of him. What was she waiting for?

"Why did you kill my son?" Luca asked. That surprised him. Luca Giovanni was not a logical, rational man. All this time, there had been an exchange of commands and threats. But not this question. This was the question any normal parent would ask. But he knew better. It was all about legitimacy to

Giovannis. He knew that because it was the same for the Moranos.

He had lost his true heir and had had no other children; his wife had died of cancer. The seat of power would be taken away from him and given to the next in line, to one of his nephews, a slap in the face of his entire existence.

"He killed my little brother." Michael said.

"You have no little brother, what are you talking about?" Luca asked.

"I did," Michael said, his tears escaping his eyes despite his control, "not in blood, but through something even greater," Michael said.

For the first time, Michael saw tears in Luca Giovannis eyes.

Maybe he did love his son.

"Blood for blood, Morano," he said. "You killed my son."

Michael stared him in the face.

"YOU KILLED MY SON!"

Luca struck his face.

Michael turned to look him in the face again. All this while, his arms were held back by Giovanni's men. And he was powerless to stop what happened next.

"I will kill you," he said, again with that dangerously silent voice. But Michael knew better. Luca Giovanni, indestructible, impenetrable lord of sin, and head of the Giovanni mafia, had been hurting all this time.

He took out his gun and placed the muzzle of its barrel on Michael's forehead. Michael closed his eyes, his last thoughts those of Hanna, Patricia, Patrick, and old man Osborne.

He knew guns. Had known them his whole life. He knew what went through the mechanism when somebody pulled the trigger. He had been on both the sides of this exchange.

And yet, no sound came.

Instead, there was a murmur coming in from the outside.

Frustrated by his lack of control, Giovanni renewed his strength on the gun, pressing it harder into Michael's forehead. But there it was again, the murmur from the outside. It was getting stronger now.

"What is that?" Giovanni said, finally having give in to his irritation.

One of the men went by a window nearby to look. "It, it's a helicopter, sir."

"A what?"

As it approached closer, the whirlwind of the helicopter increased tenfold. There was too much noise for them to hear anything but the constant whirring of the buffeting aircraft.

Bedi. It had to be Bedi.

Giovanni's men were backing up, breaking the circle they had so ceremoniously built around, watching his assassination as if it were a spectacle at a zoo.

"Cowards!" Giovanni screamed.

Before they knew it, a barrage of bullets burst throw the wooden walls, tearing away and find their home in the first pound of flesh each found. Michael got to his feet and ran for cover, ducking behind wrack of heavy machinery and equipment.

DHIK DHIK DHIK DHIK DHIK.

It was a massacre.

From the position behind the stand that Michael was in, he could see everything. Half of Giovanni's men had run. Or maybe a few? More than most, Michael was certain, had been skewered by the raining bullets.

"Holy…" Michael couldn't get the words out. But what did come was a smirk.

Where the heck was Giovanni? He suddenly realized he had lost him.

The firing stopped and Michael slowly made his way to the middle of the room, the right side of which was exposed to a cloudless blue sky and a gigantic, hovering helicopter. The wind was so strong he could barely open his eyes. His hair and clothes were a billowing mess. He waved at the pilot seat once. The helicopter turned, allowing for Michael to see Corbin standing in the passenger area.

"HEY!" He shouted over the noise. "Did we get them all?"

"NO. Giovanni got away!" Michael screamed back at him.

"What?" The idiot couldn't hear him. Michael huffed a laugh and motioned with his hands *to land the helicopter.* He saw Corbin turn around to whoever was in the passenger seat. It had to be Xavier as far as he could tell. Unless, Parvati worked out on her biceps. He couldn't really see.

Where they hell had they gotten a helicopter. It was obviously military grade. Perhaps Parvati had chipped in after all.

But where was she?

The helicopter went further up, reducing some one the noise it was previously creating. But no all of it. Xavier was planning on landing it on the roof. Given the condition the abandoned factory was now in, they would need to move inside the helicopter quickly.

His family.

Michael limped, he realized he had got to the middle of the room on limping alone, towards the exit.

A gun clicked.

"Don't you dare move, Morano."

It was Giovanni. Shit…

He was really dead this time.

"Say your prayers, you will need the in hell."

Luca's left side had been punctured with multiple bullet wounds. He was still bleeding. His suit and pants were a disaster, as was the left side of his face. It was a wonder, indeed, how the bullets had hit him no where fatal.

Or maybe they had.

BAM!

Michael opened his eyes, not realizing he had closed them yet again.

Giovanni fell on his knees, gun still in hand.

Resilient bastard.

"DIE!" He bellowed, raising his gun to aim at Michael again.

"Michael!" Michael heard someone from the door of the room.

It was Parvati.

It all happened too fast. She ran to him, jumping in an FBI maneuver and throwing at him, what Michael realized a bit too later, a gun. Michael kept his concentration on the floating firearm more than he needed to, because he heard, from one of his ears—he wasn't sure which one, again, this fight had done quiet a number on him—yet another bullet fired from Giovanni's gun.

He skid sideways, midair, holding out his cupped hands to catch the gun.

The bullet went flying away, inches from his chest.

Michael, airborne, aimed the gun at his enemy and shot. The bullet went straight through Giovanni's stone-cold heart. They both fell on the ground in sync.

Michael growned, his hitting the wooden floors having gone bad.

"You alright, Morano," Parvati asked, scanning the room for any surprises, another gun poised in her hand. Giovanni sure had been one. Michael might not have survived had Parvati not lended him a hand.

"My family—"

"—I've got them," Parvati said, "we need to move, come on." She got down to lift him up.

"What? Where are they?" Michael asked.

"They are safe," Parvati said reassuring them. "They are in the chopper, where we must go, too, so hurry the *hell* up."

"Chopper? Why the chopper? We need an ambulance!" Michael was confused.

"Yes, I had said the same. Your idiotic nerd got me to bet with him. He won, so we are going to use the bloody chopper," Parvati said, taking Michael's weight up on herself with one arm around her shoulder. They began walking to the door.

Michael huffed a laugh. At least the taught you to honor your deals at the FBI, Michael thought.

"What was the bet?" Michael had to know.

"I just saved your ass back there," Parvati said. "You owe me not to ask." Michael looked at Parvati. *Damn*. Must be embarrassing.

"I'll just ask Corbin, then," Michael said, "or Xavier."

"Over my dead-body."

They made it to the roof, and the bustling winds off the helicopter were blowing their hair and clothes every which way. He saw them then. Patricia and Hanna. They were awake.

They were alive.

Parvati helped him and he took a seat next to Patricia. Time had done naught to Patricia, it was as if she had jumped to the future as she was. Hanna, sweet Hanna, was a perfect blend of his features and her mother's.

Patricia held Michael's hand and cried into his shoulder. Hanna slid closer to her mother, too conscious among the strangers around her. He will have her time with her, Michael realized. This was about them as much as it was about him. He had to be patient and gentle with his daughter.

His daughter.

"Alright, we are taking off," Xavier bellowed over the whirlwinds of the helicopter.

"Where did you get a helicopter here so fast?" Michael shouted to Parvati.

"Never doubt a high-ranking FBI agent," Parvati said.

Corbin came to assess Michael's injuries, opening up a med kit and starting his work on him. He thought about asking what had gone between him, Bedi, and Xavier and what this stupid bet was about. But he saw Parvati looking at him. She smirked at him.

And he smirked back.

He owed her a great deal.

BEDI

Parvati was waiting in the visitor's area of the hospital Xavier, Corbin, and she had planned they would drop Michael and his family off at after the EXFIL.

It was like any other mission she had been in. Only more intense. Putting two and two together was what she had been doing for a living all this time.

When she had heard Michael being ambushed, his groans upon being hit, she had quietly followed the sounds, and those of a man being dragged across stairs, to where they were coming from. She had seen the whole exchange that occurred between Luca Giovanni and Michael. When he ordered his family be taken away, that had been her cue. She hid in the shadows and had seen where they were being taken.

Taking the amateurs guarding the two had been child's play. She had then used a trick she had once seen a few seniors do at the academy. Since both Mihchael's little girl and her mother had woken up, it meant they had been under the very sedative the trick was meant for.

She had quickly explained to them that Michael's life, and theirs, was in danger and they had to do exactly as she told them.

Parvati had next taken them to Corbin and Xavier, who had returned having ditched the car that had followed them away from the factory.

She had proposed the helicopter here.

"There is a whole army of Giovanni's men up there, we need something quick," Parvati had said.

"Like what?" Corbin had asked her.

"We are not that far away from where there might be a secret military federal base. Where there might be an attack-helicopter. I need you to hack into the security," Parvati had pointed at Corbin, "and release it."

"So, you want me to hack the FBI?" Corbin said.

"Wipe that grin off your face, we need your brain right now, besides, I know you can wipe away all traces of all our involvement. No one will know that the chopper went and came back—you in or not?" Parvati had been impatient. "We don't have time to procedurally get the damn thing!"

If anything, Corbin had grinned even wider. "On one condition," he had said.

"Boy, I will knock you to the ground," Xavier had said.

"Not if I do first," Parvati had said.

"We get to ride the helicopter, for a whole hour, around the city," Corbin had said.

"Are you out of your mind? Or do you want us all to get arrested?" Parvati had said.

"Exactly," Corbin had said. He was toying with her.

After what had been a whole minute of a delay, Parvati had caved in and said, "You are a prick, but deal."

While the chopper was now safely where it belonged, the idiot had had Xavier fly them around New York City as to the highest altitude they could go. Parvati had known, by one look at Xavier, that he was ex-military. You could also tell, by the way a person stood, if they were a pilot.

No one had taken her up like that idiot kid Corbin had. She would use manipulation like he had in her line of work. For sure. For the next time a situation came where she could use it.

It had been fun, Corbin screaming into the clouds and Xavier woohoo-ing into the, well, controls. Maybe it was what she had needed all this time. To loosen up. When was the last time perfect Parvati had had fun?

She couldn't remember.

Her mission was complete. She was going to, of course, take a shower when she returned. She looked around. Corbin and Xavier stood in one corner, talking about God only knew what. While Michael was on a bench with Patricia and Hanna.

She had helped reunite a family. She felt a small sense of pride at that. In all the work she had done, rarely did she did something like this.

Even though they didn't get to arrest Giovanni for having had the senator murdered, there was enough evidence Michael had provided her that proved the Giovanni's mafias involvement in the senator's assassination.

But Michael better buckle up, for he would be doing time, definitely and sadly so, for having assassinated a political figure. Looking at the three seated as they were, she felt she was somehow responsible for them.

She would help them in any way she could. She knew some lawyers and had uncalled favors with the country's lawmakers.

It would take an act of God to set Michael free. Or a visit to the right person.

Her phone pinged and she took it out. There was one unread text.

It was Johnny.

THEY FOUND LUCA GIOVANNI'S BODY. I KNOW MORANO GOT AWAY FROM YOU, BUT WE COME BACK STRONGER WITH THIS CASE. PINNING TO GET IT FOR US.

RECEIVED: 8:29 AM

The ignorant, selfish, narcissistic bastard.

She was getting a promotion anyway after what she had come across. Michael's treasure trove of evidence had more than just Giovanni's guilt; it detailed every transaction members of the Giovanni mafia had made. There were names and places.

She was shutting the entire Giovanni legacy down and some more.

FUCK OFF, WHITEHILL.

SENT: 8:35 AM

Four Years Later...

"You can stay in the car if you want," Patricia offered him.

"No, I'll come, too," Michael said.

They both got out. People turned to look at Michael Osborne, or Michael Morano, as had been the case with the entire country's major media outlets and newspapers. It was all out. Michael had to let his secret out into the world if were to ever have a life with his family.

They were waiting for Hanna to walk out the gates of Richmond High. Their daughter had grown so much. She had taken after Michael more than she had after Patricia. They often argued about which parent their daughter had taken after.

Michael knew Hanna was more herself than either of them.

The first few weeks of court had been brutal. Michael had been arrested. But Parvati, Xavier, and Corbin had helped him every step of the way. He had found a new friend in Parvati. They often spoke on the phone. A year before today, they had had a get-together, too. It had been great seeing Xavier, Corbin, and Bedi once again. They had spent only a few hours back then, rescuing his family. Yet they were bonded forever.

He had yet to learn what deal Corbin had made with Bedi. The detective didn't seem like the type to cave in. Corbin had been able to make her. He huffed a laugh.

"What's up, honey?" Patricia asked him, tucking away a stray bunch of her behind her ear, her wedding band catching the light from the sun.

"Nothing, just reminiscing," Michael said.

In the light of all the evidence his friends had been able to provide his attorney, and all the good Michael had done with his charities over the years, the judge had proclaimed a not-so-harsh verdict. Michael had been sentenced to two years of jail time for the events that had occurred. He had, of course, taken care of all the people that had been hurt during his entaglement with Luca Giovanni as well as he could with his money.

When Michael had been let out, he had left both his past life and that Luca Giovanni had made him live behind in prison. From behind the bars had come out a new Michael. Michael Osborne.

The press had been equally trying. Patricia and Hanna often had to deal with the aftermath of being associated with him. But it had got better. With time.

Everything did.

"There she is," Patricia said, "our darling girl."

Michael smiled as Hanna came running to her parents. She hugged her mother than him. They got into their car and Hanna told them all about what had happened in school. Listening to her talking, Michael realized he was actually happy. There had been a time where he was empty on the inside. But nothing could fill one's emptiness the way love did. And he had found it. In Hanna, and Patricia.

Patricia turned the radio on and music soon filled the car. Both mother and daughter began singing along to the sound in their off-key vocals. Michael couldn't help but laugh at that.

And on they drove.

CHARACTERS

MAIN PROTAGINISTS

•   Michael Morano (26) son of Frederick Morano (deceased) of the Morano Family and member of the Blood Lords

•   Parvati Bedi, the FBI agent

MAIN ANTAGONIST

Luca Giovanni (father of Tommy Giovanni)

THE MORANO SIBLINGS IN ORDER OF AGE

•   Frederick Morano (deceased)

•   Christina Morano

•   Enzo Morano

•   Esposito Morano

•   Helga Morano

THE BLOOD LORDS

•   Loution Morano (28) Leader of the Blood Lords and son of Christina Morano and Michael's cousin

•   Joey Morano (22) Loution's brother

Enzo Morano (successor to Frederick and his first brother) and his sons:

•   Eddie Morano (21)

•   Paul Morano (22)

•   Rob Morano (18)

Esposito Morano (Frederick's second brother) and his sons:

•   Matt Morano (22)

•   John Morano (26)

Helga Morano (Frederick's second sister) and her son:

Richie Morano (19)

MICHAELS FAMILY

- Patricia Grey (mother of Michael's daughter)

- Hanna Grey (Michael and Patricias daughter)

OTHERS

- Corbin (Michael's financial assistant and friend)

- Xavier (Michael's… other kind of assistant)

- Zoey (Michael's secretary)

- Patrick Monello (16-year-old friend of Michael who OD-ed)

- Johnny Whitehill (Parvati's Partner)

- Anna Solonik (Russian gunswoman)

- Jeanette McCalvin (Michael's employee)

- Ella Grodetsky (Parvati's friend)

This book was inspired by certain events.

Darren W. Freeman

DEDICATION

For My Grandson Bela Frederick Garvey (Freeman), Sara Freeman, Joshua Freeman, Brian Freeman, Darren Freeman, Emma Freeman, and my Marie!

SPECIAL DEDICATION

Arleen Freeman, James Freeman Sr., James Freeman Jr. and James Freeman III.

Royal Creek Publishing House

2021